PURITY OR PRISON

PURITY
OR
PRISON

BY

BRUCE HUNTER

LOGOS TO RHEMA PUBLISHING
8210 E. 71st STREET #250
TULSA, OK 74133
(918) 488-9667

ISBN: 1-57502-988-x
Morris Publishing
3212 E. Hwy 30
Kearney, NE 68847
1-800-650-7888

TABLE OF CONTENTS

DEDICATION

There are three special young people I want to dedicate this book to initially—Chad, Shauna and Trent.

These are my children! Words will never be able to express how thankful I am for their continued support over the years. It all began the day they were born. Over the years they took a journey, involuntarily, that ended in their father being incarcerated and they were hurt for no reasons of their own. They suffered in ways words will not be able to express. But through this time of pain they remained true to our almighty God, their heavenly Father. They stood for godly principles, remained pure and holy and finally walked with me through the journey that would change their father's life. They shed many tears, but in so doing they can rest assured that many other children will not have to do so. They suffered through a painful divorce so others could remain in stable families. They went without to the point of living on peanut butter sandwiches, so others can learn from their father's life how to live in integrity within the business world. Chad, Shauna and Trent are now adults and succeeding within this world. But most important of all they are in love with Jesus who is their Lord, Savior and Master.

Next, I want to dedicate this book to my parents, Mom and Dad Hunter. They walked the extra mile with me! Their prayers availed much. They took collect calls from time to time just to hear my broken heart crying out for compassion that they never refused to give. They lived what God had placed deep within them—unconditional love, acceptance and forgiveness.

As parents they stood with me during the worst storm of my entire life. I could always know that when times were especially hard, within those iron fences, Dad and Mom would be on their knees praying because God would speak to them. Having parents that are in tune with the voice of God is more than an asset, it is a divine blessing from God!

Lastly, I want to turn all my attention for the writing of this book to the only one who saw fit to love me with divine characteristics—God my Father and Creator. Over the years I was a prodigal son. Within the many years of wandering from His throne room He never gave up on me. As I walked within solitary cells and maximum security holdings the love of God permeated the atmosphere within my life, assuring me that this time alone with Him would bring my life into line with His precepts. I am so thankful God never gave up on me. He is the only true example of Fatherhood. I desire to be like His Son Jesus and imitate His very ways, thoughts, beliefs, emotions and actions. I am so thankful for spiritual heritage given through His Son and taught so diligently through the Holy Spirit. My life will never be the same!

For those who have sown financially into this book may God richly bless you.

To Mark and Kathy McNutt—Thank you for your faithfulness in standing with me through all the seasons of my life.

ACKNOWLEDGMENTS

I am a debtor to Sue Reidel, my editor and publisher, of Logos to Rhema Publishing. We have a friendship built on trust. From the outset of our acquaintance Sue recognized the prophetic writings she had received from me and spoke to me about how they could be used to touch society at its very core. The time I spent in prison revealed itself in the pages of my writings and Sue could envision them in a book which would touch and challenge many that were experiencing hurts, rejections, sins and ungodly ways—like me, needing a way out of it all! Sue has become a gift from God. She definitely brings the best out of my heart and spirit.

Others have over the years made impressive contributions to this work like Jim & Barb Green, Rev. and Mrs. Paul Roach, Reverend Ric Freeman and Dr. Ronald Cottle. Through their mentorship I have grown as a godly man and an amanuensis of what God desires to have readers obtain through my books. All of these acknowledged are truly godly professionals and my humble thanks goes out to them.

Mr. and Mrs. Roy Rakestraw were leaders of a cell group that truly walked through prison with me. They wrote me every week, or as often as their cell group met. Each letter contained encouraging words from those in attendance.

Shannon Graven capably added to the book by providing diagrams within several pages.

This book began as a letter to a special friend, Laura, and became a book about my journey to wholeness. Thanks for motivating me to write words that would disclose my inner emotions, beliefs and longings for others.

My siblings, Dael, David, Marilyn and Bonnie have been an immense support throughout this journey. I know that my lifestyle of the past years hurt them, but that the new Man within me will bring healing and needed change to our mutual relationships.

For all those, too numerous to disclose, that have been a pillar of support for many years I give a heartfelt thank you. God bless each and every one of you that refused to walk away from me, but stand and stand and stand. Those that will come to know Jesus through me and grow in a deeper walk with Him in the years to come will be credited to your heavenly account.

For all those who have endorsed this book, thank you.

Jim Bakker began a journey with me those first days at El Reno that will be cherished for the rest of my life. Thank you Jim!

David and Sharon Burdine and Steve and Darlene Allan became a source of encouragement during the initial stages of indictment and then incarceration. Thank you.

The Wentzel and Jones families in South Africa wrote and communicated often. Even the Biltong the Wentzel family attempted to send me in prison, which was returned, was a thought with great inspiration behind it. Thank you all.

Much thanks to Pastors Billy Joe & Sharon Daugherty and too Bruce Edwards and Ken Weaver also.

August 10, 1998

Dear Reader:

PURITY OR PRISON...What a meaningful name for a book that addresses the problems we all face today.

These are the very problems my father had to deal with in the past—situations in which my dad found himself deeply entrenched. This book is not only Dad's personal exhortation to me, but it is the same for your life.

Readers, please do not let yourselves sink into that awful, slimy pit that the Psalmist talks about in chapter forty of Psalms. Dad unfortunately sank into it over years of living in disobedience to God's Word. I hope that the encouragement and knowledge you receive from this book, *PURITY OR PRISON*, will assist you in endeavoring to become as pure as Christ.

Read this book with humility of heart; focus your mind on the task at hand and you will truly experience the much needed spiritual foundations to living a sanctified life.

I am real proud of my dad and love him a ton!

Chad Hunter

INTRODUCTION

Upon arriving at my final destination, El Reno, Oklahoma, in the prison system, I had to address the fruit of a past lifestyle that had brought me to this horrible place. I had two options: one was to fall into a lethargical, denial mode like 95 percent of most prisoners, and somehow leave one day a poisoned, bitter, revenge-filled, convicted felon; or I could use this time to unravel those layers of a sin-filled lifestyle one at a time and allow the purging fire of God and the cleansing power of the blood of Christ to remove the diseased inner lusts once and for all!

Sin does not begin in big ways. It is subtly introduced by Satan in ways that appear so insignificant. It reminds me of the experiment I once did in high school biology classes. A frog was placed in a pan of warm water. Initially the warm water lulls the frog into insensitivity to its surroundings. But, then I placed the pan on a stove and turned the heat up slowly. The frog never moved or showed any discomfort because the water was warm and he had acclimated to it. As the water temperature increased so did the inner body temperature of the frog. Ironically, the inside temperature of the frog became like the outside temperature of the water. Initially it was not a problem, but by the time the frog noticed the severity of the temperature it was too late to jump out of the pan. Why? The frog was getting boiled in the very water that it sat comfortably in. Immunity to circumstances and conditions lulled it into compromise that eventually would cost its life.

Satan, with his devious mind and our willingness to allow him, does likewise.

Purity or Prison

As I began to consider the forty or so years of my life, there had to be a place of recognition of where I had set a place for Satan to lull me into a state of compromise that almost cost me my life. Denial would not offer me a respite from each and every wrong act. The fact that I had been sentenced to prison for financial crimes was only the tip of one massive iceberg. The fruit of my lifestyle came from a root that needed to be discovered and then dug out, chopped up into small pieces and placed on a massive bonfire for final and complete destruction!

Immunity to sinful ways comes as a thief in the night. Peter says we are to flee fleshly lusts that war against the soul (1Peter 2:11). Christ calls us out of darkness and into His marvelous light. Darkness impedes spiritual progress; it maintains one in a state of ignorance and error. But His light has virtues that are opposite to darkness. The light of God needs no kindling to become light, neither does it ever become extinguished. I want to live in that light daily! The question I pose is, do you? Satan's continuing influence and our acceptance of it in disobedience to God's Word build up within each victim an immunity to the most subtle of his devious plans to destroy us!

In a recent book written by Dr. Don Raunikar entitled ***Choosing God's Best***, he brings to light some interesting statistics. These statistics show us how sin has escalated in our nation. This nation called "One Nation Under God." On pages 40 and 41 he states the following:

* *Sex Before Marriage*

In its 1994 survey on risky behavior among young people, the Centers for Disease Control and Prevention found that more than half the high schoolers in the United States have had sex. To many Christian singles (and parents) the following breakdown will be astonishing:

Ninth grade	40%
Tenth grade	48%
Eleventh grade	57%
Twelfth grade	72%

Fifty percent of teenage girls between fifteen and nineteen years old have had sexual intercourse at least once, according to the 1995 National Survey of Family Growth, an in-depth government survey conducted every five years. In 1970, 29 percent of girls said they had sex.

By age nineteen, 86 percent of today's unmarried males have had sexual intercourse, up from 78 percent in 1979.

Forty percent of women become pregnant before they are twenty years old, giving the United States a higher teen pregnancy rate than any other industrialized nation. Half of teen pregnancies end in birth, one-third in abortion and the rest in miscarriage.

Seventy-four percent of teenagers say they would live with someone before marriage or instead of getting married.

Purity or Prison

More than 43 percent of women ages fifteen to twenty-four who gave birth in the early 1990s were not married, compared to only 14 percent in the early 1960s.

Sexually Transmitted Disease (STD)

Five known venereal diseases existed in 1950; today more than fifty different organisms and syndromes are passed sexually.

Every day, 33,000 new cases of a sexually transmitted disease are reported in America (12 million a year); one in four of the adult population has a permanent STD.

At least 30 percent of single, sexually active Americans have herpes and the herpes virus is spreading at the alarming rate of 500,000 new cases a year.

Abortion

About 1.7 million abortions are performed annually, with nearly one-eighth during the second or third trimester. Ninety-three percent of the time, no "special cases" exist such as rape or incest, health problems, or a mother whose life is threatened.

Twenty-eight hundred teenage girls get pregnant every day; 40 percent will have abortions.

Bruce Hunter

We are having a national moral breakdown and men must take responsibility before God to walk and live a pure life free from fornication and adultery if we ever hope to change this situation.

The church has become apathetic and we have been overcome with a great darkness. What began as a very simple touching of my girlfriend's breasts at sixteen developed within me an ultimate lifestyle of sexual perversion. I did feel conviction and after numerous occasions of being familiar with this girl I attempted to seek counsel from my pastor. He laughed at me and shared that as long as I was not having sex that those types of events were normal occurrences for a young man like me.

His blessing appeared evident as I proceeded to develop an inner hunger for her sexually. Over time those persistent actions, sanctioned by my Pastor, fueled my lust and drove me to fulfill my desires in disobedience to God.

It is my prayer that you will read this book, see my journey from purity to prison and take immediate steps to come back into a right relationship with God and your loved ones.

A man who remains stiff-necked after many rebukes
will suddenly be destroyed—without remedy.
Proverbs 29:1

Darkness impedes spiritual progress; it maintains one in a state of ignorance and error.

PRELUDE

It was a drizzly, cold day in May, 1996 just a few days before Mother's Day. As I walked despondently across the grassy knolls of El Reno prison my heart cried out to God. There would be no real celebration for me again this Mother's Day. My mother had gone to be with our Lord in 1978. My marriage had crumbled under the heavy weight of my sinful lifestyle. Not even the thought of being able to celebrate it with my own children's mother was possible. At that point self-pity began to enthrone itself and boot God off the throne of my life.

Prison at those special times of the year is indescribable. The vacancy within you can numb you from even considering a joyful disposition. As I walked there appeared in front of me some spring flowers. There were three about the size of my thumb beautifully dressed in purple. They looked like tulips.

"Pick them and take them to your cell!"

This voice spoke with definitive resolution. At once I was aware of the Holy Spirit speaking. As I walked by these little wonders of His majestic creation the voice repeated itself. Within me a questioning rose up. "What am I going to do with them?" Then He spoke to me to take one along with a feather lying on the ground nearby to a lady staff member. THAT WAS OUTRAGEOUS!

Things like that were a sign of caving in to the administration. It was also a signal to the inmates that I was selling out and possibly becoming a snitch.

Purity or Prison

For a few minutes I debated the issue with myself and God. This was no easy request in a place like El Reno! I thought about the advantages and disadvantages and the disadvantages were winning in my mind. Surely, God would not ask me to do this. The urging was so strong I decided not to fight it and I picked the flowers. I proceeded to return to my cell because the 4 o'clock count time was about to occur. As I walked into the cell the flowers were held sheepishly on my part. Now, I felt the Holy Spirit speak to me again. "Give each of my two cell mates a flower." As I did a strength I had rarely felt spoke an illustration through me to my cell mates. I told them how to trust God for all their provisions and clothing just like these beautiful creations do. It became a great object lesson and we all gleaned a greater understanding of God's care for us in this place. The real test came after count time.

This lady staff member, Cindy is what I will name her, was in her office for she worked late every Wednesday. The only problem was her office was across from the chow hall and her door had a glass window in it through which the inmates could look. I knocked and she beckoned me to enter. Words began to roll out of my mouth right from the heart of God, "Cindy, God has called on me in an unusual way to give you this beautiful little flower and bird feather. The Holy Spirit is telling me to encourage you to go ahead and marry the man you are now dating. God wants you to be his wife. The flower represents how God will clothe your marriage with such harmony, peace and joy. The feather reveals that He will provide for each and every need more supernaturally than He does for the birds of the field."

Those words flowed out of my mouth as though pre-planned, but truly they were not my own.

Then it all happened and an alarm went off inside of me. Cindy began to cry. I stood there in absolute shock. What would the inmates think seeing her crying in the office? Worse yet, what would happen if a guard came past and saw her weeping? My heart sank into my boots, and I wanted to run and hide.

Then she spoke, "Bruce, God sent you to do this today. You are an angel sent from above. I have been engaged to this man for some time now, but there has become of recent days a real doubt within me that this marriage would work. He has three children and the devil has been playing tricks with my mind. He has been saying it will never work. His voice has been spreading doubt within me that I would be a failure as a stepmother. As a result I had decided today to break it off. Now you come along and share godly encouragement. It must be God's will to marry him. Thank you for being obedient to the voice of the Holy Spirit. May I hold onto this flower and feather and keep them as momentos of your words?"

"Of course," I agreed. I left her office with such an inner joy at being able to be used by God in such a unique and unusual way. But that is not the end to this little story. On Sunday in chapel the minister asked to have inmates stand and share a testimony about Mother's Day and what it meant to them. My Spanish speaking cell mate, Nacho, stood. He shared about the little flower I gave him on the preceding Wednesday. Then he went on to share how a Spanish brother came into the cell that same night and saw the flower.

Purity or Prison

Nacho gave it to him to send to his wife inside of a card. The brother was thrilled for his wife lived in Mexico and had not received a present or anything from him. Praise God, this beautiful little flower from the prison in El Reno warmed the heart of a precious Mexican mother while her husband was far away from her.

How could I be so sensitive to hearing His voice? How was I able to identify the real voice and pursuing will of God? Over the years that was so difficult. Prison had become a place in which my spiritual ears became sensitized to the voice of the Holy Spirit. To learn how to identify God's voice is important. Without ears to hear the things of the Spirit of God our walk with Him is just carnal at best and disobedient at its very worst.

There are some important issues God had me learn while I was incarcerated in El Reno. This book you are about to read will provide acorns of truth about God's love, grace and mercy. It is my prayer that they would be buried into your heart and grow into mighty oak trees in your life.

I have learned a great lesson from having my freedom removed. Life consists of learning to obey the "Master's voice." It is a school of training each and every day. I had to take a long and hard look at the reality check of prison in my life and realize I had not obeyed the voice of God and there was a day of reckoning in my life.

This book should help you learn to hear God's voice in your life also. It doesn't have to take a physical or spiritual prison to learn the lessons. They can be learned if you have a teachable spirit and will confess your sins and ask forgiveness of an awesome God.

1 LESSONS LEARNED THE HARD WAY ARE NEVER GOD'S WAY

On June 6, 1992, I spent my first day in prison! To write about my life is difficult, but I believe the Holy Spirit is inspiring me to write plainly and help others avoid the decisions I made. I had been deceived by Satan for so many years I now know how easy it is to run from reality and blame the evil one for all one's misfortunes thereby failing to claim FULL RESPONSIBILITY for my actions and decisions. My first day in prison was also the day my journey to wholeness and truth began.

While my family and I prepared for my eldest son's high school graduation in Springfield, Missouri, two law enforcement officers of the FBI walked up to me at the ceremony's arena. My life suddenly took on a new dimension as I heard one of the FBI agents say, "Bruce Hunter, I have a warrant for your arrest! You can either come willingly without any incident before it begins, or we will have no option but to wrestle you to the floor and take you by force."

My life felt like a precious porcelain vase having been knocked off the shelf onto a tile floor below; shattered, wounded and irreversibly destroyed with no hope of sanity or purpose.

My corporate, pinstriped suit became replaced, in what seemed like moments, with an orange jumpsuit.

Purity or Prison

My fingers that had once held millions of dollars and clasped the hands of powerful men now pressed across a black ink pad. I became known as 06883-045. Forever and an age, it would seem, as I was merely a number to those sent to strip me of my sinful ways that had held me to a lifestyle of seeming prosperity and success. The two-man concrete cell became claustrophobic as my mind escalated into painful disarray. A deep, frantic fear took over as I saw a lack of control slipping through my fingers.

How could a Christian, a missionary's son with a call to preach, ever encounter the wrong side of the law? What seeds were sown over the years that could possibly lead to such massive destruction and ultimately shatter a marriage of twenty-one years? How could a father have done something so wrong that would batter, bruise and devastate three beautiful teenage children? What ungodly decisions could a businessman have made to hurt friends, banks and shareholders? These would be questions I would be required to answer over time—for somewhere below the surface would surely lay the answers of truth.

"Behold, thou desirest TRUTH in the inward parts: and in the hidden part thou shalt make me to know wisdom" (Psalm 51:6).

As I truly began to unravel the known sins within my life, God was faithful to then release the hidden sins and dysfunctions that had for so many years overtaken me. Satan comes to steal your joy, kill the Word and then destroy your reconciling capabilities. You must ask for forgiveness, give forgiveness, and receive forgiveness in order to be reconciled to God and man.

If you do not understand the reconciling blood of Jesus then Satan has won the battle and eternal death is his plan for you. If you fail to see Jesus' blood and forgiveness, you will never understand the power to overcome sin. Then Satan relaxes your spiritual senses and requires you to live an impulsive lifestyle. But praise God, the blood, the Word and the name of Jesus are still active and even in prison His unconditional love still reached out to a sinner like me.

Over the past forty-nine years so much had happened within my life. If only the answers I have today would have been more accessible to me during the most important years of my adulthood I could have avoided the pain, sorrow and suffering that God never had planned or wanted me to experience. He only wanted me to experience the good not the evil. It was my conscious choices to choose death over life, curses instead of blessings that ultimately landed me behind iron bars of steel.

During the dark, lonely hours of that first night in a cold, gray, concrete, county jail cell, my past lifestyle of sinful carnage and debauchery flashed before my eyes. I fell prostrate on the floor, and with a repentant spirit and soul, cried out to God for help. The sin that had become entrenched within my life over the years reminded me of the many rings found within an onion; one small inner ring is consistently surrounded by layers of increasingly larger outer rings. When the knife of correction was put to my life, like the onion when cut, it produced a stream of tears. A purging of both spirit and soul would be needed to break through the years of sin upon sin, until I would be presentable as a vessel for His use.

There would be no artificial bandages able to heal and scourge these sinful wounds.

Only time and painful, persistent, truthful inner reflection on my part would correct evil habits that had permeated my character. Satan's tentacles that entwined my soul would have to be broken and destroyed forever.

Disobedience to God's Word in the area of sexual morality was a big step in the sinful lifestyle that walked me into this cell. No, I did not physically rape or molest anyone, but by participating in prostitution, and an unsavory lifestyle my imagination and mind were raped and pillaged by Satan and turned over to demonic, lustful thoughts. I had disobeyed the warning given to us in 1 Corinthians 6: 13-20 KJV:

"...Now the body is not for fornication, but for the Lord; and the Lord for the body. And God hath both raised up the Lord, and will also raise up us by his own power. Know ye not that your bodies are the members of Christ? shall I then take the members of Christ, and make them the members of an harlot? God forbid. What? know ye not that he which is joined to an harlot is one body? for two, saith he, shall be one flesh. But he that is joined unto the Lord is one spirit. FLEE FORNICATION. EVERY SIN THAT A MAN DOETH IS WITHOUT THE BODY; BUT HE THAT COMMITTETH FORNICATION SINNETH AGAINST HIS OWN BODY. What? know ye not that your body is the temple of the Holy Ghost which is in you, which ye have of God, and ye are not your own?

For ye are bought with a price: therefore glorify God in your body, and in your spirit, which are God's."

I chose, like many reading this book, to ignore this pleading of the Lord, to my own detriment.

If we take a look at the teenage pregnancy and divorce in this country we can see where sexual immorality leads us—abortion, murder, lust, perversion and a total lack of peace. A tormented mind that can only be restored by the complete act of repentance, the blood of Christ, the forgiveness offered and the POWER of the Holy Spirit working in you daily! Praise God, there is total and complete deliverance waiting for you just as there was for me.

Many reading this book have walked in the same shoes as I did in so many ways. Old prisoners say, "Been there and done that!" Even the footprints in the sands of your life have familiar tread, size and direction. That is why I have an unction from The Holy One to write this prophetic warning to a generation who no longer understands the concept of virginity for a man and a woman according to God's Word.

Some of what will be shared in this book comes with experiential knowledge while some of it comes from prophetic manifestation. Both, however, come from a man who dearly cares for you and desires more than anything to see you walk in relationship to God (our Father) in reconciliation, restoration, renewal and divine wholeness before it is too late. Precious time is allocated daily in intercession for you, the reader, so that you may grasp the great truth of sexual morality before it is too late!

Purity or Prison

The mere fact God has allowed this book to be placed into your hands lets me know you are at the most important CROSSROADS of your life.

You are about to embark upon a journey of understanding God's perfect will for your life and you will be brought to a PLACE OF DECISION.

I was born and raised in Johannesburg, South Africa, the son of Pentecostal missionaries. As a young child I remember being about eight years old and my father taking me on a roller coaster for the first time in my life. It truly was one of the most horrific experiences I have ever encountered. I screamed, yelled, cried, begged to get off, but there was nothing that could be done until the ride ended. At the time of my arrest I remembered vividly that wild, frightening ride and I knew prison would be far worse than that youthful memory. Fear grabbed hold of me like a lion puts a stranglehold on its prey.

When Satan deceives you into a sexually immoral lifestyle you don't know it but you have been strapped in for a wild ride. From the very minute you decided to enter into sexual intimacy outside of marriage you were sidetracked by Satan and you turned to the left and the right in your relationship with God.

An immoral lifestyle takes away:
HIS PRECIOUS MOMENTS FOR YOU TO IMPACT OTHERS FOR ETERNITY'S SAKE.

However, I want to encourage you—what Satan meant for your harm, God can turn to your good.

You are a person who has a great destiny awaiting you. Out of the rubble of heartache will come a supernatural life rising above it all.

Spiritual understanding from the Holy Spirit as teacher combined with Agape Therapy is the most predictable of all counseling tools.

Agape Therapy is godly, unconquerable, benevolence, invincible goodwill that results in reconciliation, renewal, health, wholeness and maturity in one's walk with God. The symptoms, once recognized, truly reveal the root to all the fruit. God's word never fails to provide answers for the hurting symptoms but more importantly it introduces His plan on how to remove the root causes for eternal purposes. The bottom line is you and I must be willing to deal with the hurt and the root causes with a spirit of CONVICTION and a HEART OF REPENTANCE! Too often over the years prior to prison my spirit would be convicted and I would repent. But I was like Judas. My repentance was out of an embarrassment because I **"GOT CAUGHT."**

When Peter repented from denying Christ, the Greek word was *metanoia*. This unique word means he turned 180 degrees and never did it again! His repentance came according to the Word because he remembered the words of Jesus. He had sinned greatly but he came back to complete acceptance and forgiveness through his repentant attitude.

JUDAS' REPENTANCE ENDED IN SUICIDE! Peter, after his repentance, preached his first sermon and won 3,000 souls to Christ!

Purity or Prison

The UNCONDITIONAL love of Jesus will cause you to be blessed. You may not be in a physical prison cell, but many are locked away in their body and soul to a sexually impure spirit that is robbing every blessing of life and God from them.

True repentance will be like Peter, *metanoia*, a 180 degree turn never experiencing that sin again. It is then and only then that you can live in the supernatural realm of **power, love** and **a sound mind**.

2 UNCONDITIONAL LOVE

One of the greatest purposes in writing this book is to let you know that God loves you with a divine, unconditional acceptance and love. Regardless of your past His love for you sees beyond forgiving through the blood of Jesus. Who am I to cast the first stone at anyone? More importantly, I desire to speak the truth to you in love through this book of restoration. I hope to discuss sensitive matters in such a way that you will see how God has taken me from an all-out sinner to His throne of grace and mercy. He will do the same for you. By knowing and understanding His reconciling heart and character I am free to share the details of my life without the shock, alarm or the withdrawing that used to take place in my life.

Because of my complete and total belief in the forgiveness of sins I know this book and the reading of it will be funneled through a heart that sees you as a child of the King of kings and with the expressed desire to protect you as I deal with the subject of sexuality. God wants you and me to refrain from any sexual, physical contact outside of marriage! He does not desire you to be wounded, broken and diseased. Godliness in your own life and in your personal relationships is of the utmost importance. Peter calls on you to be **HOLY** as **God is HOLY!**

As I stated in the previous chapter I was born in Johannesburg, South Africa, to missionary parents. As a young child I knew God called me to the fivefold ministry.

Purity or Prison

Over the years my life had taken so many detours that His ways seemed foreign to me.

In my prison cell God in His wonderful mercy reminded me, **"God's gifts and His call are irrevocable"** (Romans 11:29). Undoubtedly this prison wilderness was God's last appeal to me to obey Him and redirect my life.

The months after the arrest became a painful downward spiral encompassing every area of my life. My wife divorced me after twenty-one years of marriage, my three teenage children were tragically wounded and hurt, all financial stability was lost, friends despised me, relatives looked on with jaundiced eyes and rejection and loneliness set in while the federal prosecutors and the FBI in Dallas and Denver began their journey to successful prosecution.

When I was in the pit of despair and considering suicide my lawyer called and proceeded to explain the twenty-two counts against me over the phone. "Bruce, the Grand Jury materials are here, and I have reviewed some of it. It looks very bad! I cannot help you. First, there are at least fifteen counts on which you will be found guilty. Second, I am in the middle of a murder trial and have been paid $50,000 to represent the defendant. You know that the court pays all my legal fees to represent you and it is insignificant compared to the fee I have earned in this murder trial. Bruce, you will have to come to Colorado and sift through all this material and build your own case. In the end you could be sentenced to forty years in prison."

In utter despair I hung up the phone. It was like being given a death sentence!

Within me every soulful feeling seemed lower than a snake's belly in a wagon track. It appeared there would be no forgiveness or mercy from the government.

I love what Isaiah says in chapter 1, verses 18 through 20, *"Come now, and let us reason together, saith the Lord: though your sins be as scarlet, they shall be as white as snow; though they be red like crimson, they shall be as wool. If ye be WILLING and OBEDIENT, ye shall eat the GOOD of the land: But if ye REFUSE and REBEL, ye SHALL BE DEVOURED by the sword: for the mouth of the Lord hath spoken it."*

YOU MUST BELIEVE IN HIS COMPLETE FORGIVENESS TO UNDERSTAND HIS UNCONDITIONAL LOVE.

He sees us as complete virgins when we repent and turn completely from our debauched lifestyle. He sees you as one with holiness and integrity, but most importantly He sees you through the blood of Jesus having all the stains and scars of a sinful life totally and completely washed away! I came to the place of complete repentance and turned my entire being over to the mercy and forgiveness of the Lord.

One week later I arrived at my lawyer's office in Colorado Springs. He ushered me into his office with a confidently assuring smile, then uttered these words; "Bruce, you are a miracle man. In over twenty years of criminal defense I have never had a prosecutor come to me one week before a trial, especially when the charges are bonafide, and seek a plea bargain. Bruce, this prosecutor is willing to drop all charges if you will select any two, plead guilty on those two immediately this week."

This was a miracle! Only God could get credit for having done all this. I faced the judge that fateful day, recognizing God's hand in the affairs of my life, and was sentenced to eight years and five months in a federal prison. However, that's not where it ended. Five months after arriving in prison, officers with the Justice department met with me and reduced my sentence an additional forty months. PRAISE GOD! I know when I wept before God and begged for forgiveness over an immoral lifestyle He heard me and forgave me and started the process of deliverance in my life.

If you have never experienced a sexual relationship this book will serve as a great BLESSING to you and a WARNING. You are truly in a place where God can impart to you all the wonderful blessings of love and marriage. **STAY PURE! You are in a tremendous place with the Lord.**

If you have entered into sexual relations outside of marriage, like myself, you have sinned before God. Hopefully, like myself, you will read and come to a place of conviction, remorse, repentance and knowledge of **GOD'S UNCONDITIONAL LOVE. It is this kind of love that saves, forgives, heals, delivers and gives us hope for a future!** God loves us. He wants us to speak truth in the innermost being and He wants the truth out of us in the hidden parts.

It is imperative you see yourself restored to virginity!

I will explain the importance of this in the next chapter and I believe the truth the Lord has shown me will **CHANGE YOUR LIFE!**

The Holy Spirit does not want our relationship to be filled with lustful longings, but one in which we hold each other accountable to the Word and character of God. Our relationships are founded on the Rock, Christ Jesus, where the spiritual side is emphasized, and the soul ties introduced with Holy Spirit inspiration. His Word, counsel and helpful Christian resource books guide us into further intimacy with God and proper, healthy, loving relationships with each other.

I believe this book will assist you in coming back to a profound and intimate relationship with God, keep you from making the mistakes I made, and restore godly character back to the body of Christ. Jesus never meant for me to spend one day in prison. It was after I was incarcerated that I realized through God's tender dealings with me that my immoral lifestyle had caused me to be imprisoned long before I became 06883-045.

As you relate to this new and exciting adventure of **PURITY** you will find a **joy unspeakable and full of glory**. My life yearns to bless you and be a godly influence to you through the writing of this book.

Intercession is at the core of it, the writing of it, and the delivery. Intercession is also over you as you read.

As I truly began to unravel the known sins within my life,

Purity or Purpose

God was faithful to then release the hidden sins and dysfunctions that had for so many years overtaken me.

Satan comes to steal your joy, kill the Word and destroy your life. God comes to heal, deliver, set free and FORGIVE.

You may be overcome with great emotional sorrow and grief as you read this book and surprisingly find yourself between the pages. Don't short-circuit the work of God in your life. Let the sorrow come, let the tears flow, grieve for what Satan has stolen from you and then come to **complete repentance**. The kind Peter found, and then win souls, save lives, train young men in truth and be a part of the wonderful Kingdom of God and His Unconditional Love!

3 MAN'S VIRGINITY— THE FOUNDATION FOR HOLY MATRIMONY

A man's virginity is the absolute will of God for your life! Men, I know that you are not used to hearing this, but the greatest robbery of your future is losing your virginity! The greatest loss, the ability to truly love a woman is stolen from you the minute you lose your virginity outside of marriage! The entire structure of marriage according to what God has planned for His Body is dependent on the virginity of men and women.

MEN, YOU MUST REMAIN A VIRGIN TO EXPERIENCE TRUE LOVE BETWEEN A HUSBAND AND WIFE.

On my journey to recovery and forgiveness the Holy Spirit allowed a tremendous book to come into my hands. It is called, *Why The Hymen* by Shelia Cooley. In Ms. Cooley's book some profound revelations about sexual covenants are revealed. It is must reading for men as well as women.

One of the saddest aspects to fornication is how Satan totally deceives the parties involved. It is very difficult for anyone to believe they are walking in deception, but if you are in a relationship that is sexual and you are not married **YOU ARE DECEIVED!** Without a doubt I can say your relationship that is sexual outside of marriage is not the perfect will of God.

Purity or Prison

It is not the will of God at all. It is inundated with massive, Satanic deception and doomed for failure regardless of your church attendance and spiritual acumen and in some cases the ultimate desire for a ministry! This deception, to think you could enter into the sin of fornication, completely forbidden by God, and have God's blessing is a **GREAT LIE**! As Satan beguiled Eve he has done the same to you if you think you are the exception to the Word of God and partake of that which God has forbidden outside of marriage.

Deception started like a spot of mold on bread. If kept secret or in the dark, pretty soon that spot of mold completely covers the bread. **Sexual sin is like the mold of life.** When we try to witness to others and offer them help, they see a moldy piece of bread—**your sinful life**—that you see as pure because you have been deceived. You wonder why you have not won many to Christ, they have no problem seeing clearly that you have been blinded by Satan too.

The following is from Ms. Cooley's book,

"For even hereunto were ye called: because Christ also suffered for us, leaving us an example, that ye should follow his steps: WHO DID NO SIN..." (1Peter 2:21,22).

"Jesus presented Himself without sin: clean, holy, and acceptable. This tells us that through His death, and by His blood, Jesus entered into the Holy of Holies. There, He presented His shed blood on the altar, to forever be a sacrifice for our sins, able to be seen clean and spotless before the Father. Jesus had to be sin free.

If Jesus had sinned just one time, He could not have gone to the Holy of Holies on our behalf.

He could not have entered the Holy of Holies to present His blood. Now, through the very blood that Jesus shed, we can be born again and enter into a new covenant with the Father God.

Therefore, it should be established within the hearts of young men, that each one should present himself to that new blood covenant without sin or blemish, undefiled, holy and acceptable, a virgin in his manhood: a "Prince Charming" to a virgin, and enter the blood covenant of marriage.

Jesus is coming for His bride and **He is undefiled, without sin. So also, the man should meet his bride at the altar sexually undefiled, without any other sexual covenant!** Coming to the altar as an undefiled man, he is giving to his wife the greatest gift he will ever or could ever give her, **THE TOTAL MAN**: SPIRIT, SOUL AND BODY!

"Husbands, love your wives, even as Christ also loved the church, and gave himself for it" (Ephesians 5:24). *

Men, once you enter into sexual relations outside of marriage you are defiled, full of sin, and there is no way you can come to the altar and enter the marriage covenant with the blessing of God. There is absolutely no way to love your wife like Christ loved the church! **The minute Satan robs your virginity he has stolen the whole foundation for holy matrimony.**

No wonder marriage can be hell, even for the believers who have entered into this compromised lifestyle. Satan holds the reigns of lust over your life and he signed the contract for a marriage with a spirit of lust, fornication, and eventually adultery to rule and reign over the marriage.

Is there hope? Yes, Yes, Yes. God's unconditional love when we turn to Him in complete repentance! Then and only then can we become the virgin God commanded us to be because we are **reconciled, redeemed, forgiven and seen white as snow before Him.**

As I began my prison journey I was looking for answers to questions I was asking myself. What caused me to abandon my virginity with such foolish and determined recklessness? Why would I just allow an impulse to control my life to the point of risking possible death through some loathsome disease? Where did my secret and sinful ways come from? I began an honest search for the truth to these questions. I needed the answers because if left to myself my eventual release would only unleash an undetected, manipulative and compulsive appetite for more immorality and I knew it could never be satisfied. It drove me. I had to change. I had to find the answers. I knew I was finally ready to listen.

Being raised by missionary parents I took an approach I felt my father would speak to me. He would ask me a straightforward question and he would expect a straight-forward answer. His question would be:
What would occur to me eternally if I did not change such wicked living?

The Bible is quite clear on the consequences of immoral living, *"Now the works of the flesh are manifest, which are these; adultery fornication, uncleanness, lasciviousness, idolatry, witchcraft, hatred,...and such like: of the which I tell you before, as I have also told you in time past, that THEY WHICH DO SUCH THINGS SHALL NOT INHERIT THE KINGDOM OF GOD"* (Galatians 5:19-21). *"Know ye not that the unrighteous shall not inherit the kingdom of God? Be not deceived: neither fornicators, nor idolaters, nor adulterers...shall inherit the kingdom of God"* (1 Corinthians 6:9,10).

Wow! What a revelation. Sinful living in sexual ways will end in eternal imprisonment far from the presence of God. Going to prison physically isolates an inmate from loved ones and friends. It was emotionally the most sorrowful experience of my life. But physical imprisonment cannot begin to compare with being removed from God's presence for eternity.

As I contemplated these verses, questions of why I became so sinful took on a greater demand for answers. Roots of wicked perversion had to be dug out, cut up and burned. Paul tells us in the scriptures, *"Our God is a consuming fire"* (Hebrews 12:29). I wanted His fire to consume the roots of immorality. When I took the "T" of the cross of Christ into my life I could make the word IMMORALITY translate into the life of IMMORTALITY! I wanted to live free of immorality and gain Christ's immortality.

Lust was part of the flesh of my life. Jesus wanted to give me hope.

Purity or Prison

What is lust? Lust demands immediate gratification without any delay.

What is hope? Hope is a godly desire for something with an expectation that it will happen.

Lust victimizes the very core of a person through compulsion and habits that eventually become bondage to them. **Hope actualizes God's purpose and grace within your life and helps you walk in holiness and purity. HOPE will never fail you. LUST WILL DESTROY YOU.**

Lust is a demonic force. **Hope is from the throne room of God.**

Lust ends in death. **Hope ends in life.**

Lust steals your purity and prevents grace to flow to you or others. **Hope and the love of God make you a giver of grace.** His love helps you to live in love, acceptance and forgiveness.

Lust victimizes people. When relationships are bathed in jaundiced and soured lustfulness, there is a process that cannot be avoided. You begin to prey on the weaknesses of others. You pick up a pimp nature that prostitutes your victims to your habits and desires. **Hope blesses, encourages and strengthens others.** It is the Samaritans law of "do unto others as you would have others do unto you," put into practice.

Lust is used by Satan to destroy your character. It steals your joy, peace, finances and the very stability of your soul.

Hope gives you a Christlike character that has honesty and integrity as its very foundation. It comes to create a good life for you and gives you a future.

Lust demands immediate gratification. It cannot be delayed.

Hope is a desire for something and a belief God will bring it in the perfect timing to be a blessing in your life.

Lust produces a floundering lifestyle. Lust seeks no definition, is self-centered, directionless and is determined to have its own way. It produces a double minded man and fills a person with deception. Lust brings shame and blame with inevitable self-centered decisions. This will lead to lying, stealing and hate-filled ways.

Hope will never allow shame and guilt to rob you of a place in God's kingdom. The love of God when it is shed forth in your heart and mine will bring us into a cleansed state and we will live an abundant life.

Lust will ruin your life if left unchecked.

You can run from this message and pretend you are not guilty or you can admit your sins and start a process of healing in your life.

Purity or Prison

Your lifestyle may look picture perfect because all is hidden with the archives of the past. Over the years history has proven to me that everything I attempted to gain through lust not only was temporal, but revealed its wicked head in due season. Lust remains in a cyclical form if it is not dealt with. The cycle goes something like this. You're tempted, nurturing that lustful thinking, conceiving it with evil deeds, leading you into open rebellion. Soon and very soon sin will bring a darkness of death in your life. I urge you to flee from fornication and every evil way.

I choose to live with the hope of God. Why? When I attach it to the faith of Jesus Christ, my Lord and Master, the cleansing, forgiveness and future I want for myself and others is more than possible; it is promised. This hope brings me into a right standing with Almighty God. It assures me of peace, joy, love, life and abundant life.

God has promised when we confess our sins to Him that He will:

> **Wash Us**—The blood of Christ makes us white as snow.

> **Sanctify Us**—We are set aside as an holy heir with Jesus.

> **Justify Us**—Treated by God as though sinful lusts had never existed in our lives.

What a tremendous victory can be experienced when Christ becomes the dominant force in your life. Lust dissipates into the abyss of darkness and the light of God takes its place filling you with His holiness and purity.

Yes, you can live in victory over lusts. Just apply the blood of Jesus and the power of His name each and every time temptations begin to knock at the door of your heart. I was physically locked up when I came to my senses, but in that prison I became the most liberated human being on the face of the earth. I was set free from this sexual bondage and now I have peace that passes all understanding! You can have this freedom too. Its yours if you will yield yourself to the blood of Jesus and the power of His Word.

Mican Kundera states, "The first betrayal is irreparable. It calls forth a chain reaction of further betrayals, each of which takes us farther and farther away from the point of our original betrayal."

*Shelia Cooley. <u>WHY THE HYMEN</u> Tulsa, OK: Logos To Rhema Publishing, Copyright © 1997, pp 3-7.
(Information on how to obtain this book is given at the back of this book.)

4 THE "THEOS"

In 1970, I arrived in the United States with $300 and a vision to attend seminary and then return to South Africa to become a part of spreading the Gospel to that apartheid nation. Within a few short years the love of money and a desire to become rich brought temptations that would ensnare my actions. This striving desire, energized and motivated many foolish and hurtful lusts that eventually ushered in a flood of destruction. I had become the president of a public company with varied illegal and fraudulent dealings with banks and savings and loans within Texas and Colorado.

U. S. Attorneys in both states served me with twenty-two counts of indictment for financial fraud. My sentence had the potential to carry over eighty years in the federal penitentiary. The stark reality of dying in prison stared me in the face. I was petrified, wounded and not sure I could survive this new environment. I would soon learn God's grace is sufficient and truly in my weakness He would become my strength. As prison life began, a tugging in my heart ensued. I would be the sole decision-maker as to how prison life would impact my life. Would repentance and a purging come forth, or would bitterness and despair prevail?

My decision was to seek the face of God. I sought holiness, love, faithfulness, humility, thankfulness and contentment each and every day.

I knew these traits would reflect and exalt the character of God. I began studying the lives of prophets like Ezekiel. It became obvious to me that Ezekiel's name, which means "God strengthens," was realized during his time of captivity. God allowed Ezekiel during his captivity to experience spiritual revelations. God revealed himself in intimate ways to me, as I recklessly abandoned my spirit and soul totally to Him.

Over the years a sowing of false thoughts, ungodly beliefs, unstable emotions and ungodly actions had embedded themselves into a character that reflected inner ways influenced by Satan and externalized in ways totally displeasing to God and man. Destiny will always reveal itself in time—good or bad. I determined, like Ezra, to study God's Word and become a willing and obedient vessel.

Any relationship that is headed for marital bliss MUST BE WITHIN GODLY COVENANT. God is never out of order when it comes to His will, Word and pre-ordained purpose for our lives. Through the Word there is a set order to covenant making.

The word that stands for God in the Greek is THEOS. It has five letters and each letter acts as an acronym detailing the plans God lays out for divine covenant making.

"T" **Transcendent:** Anytime we want to get into covenant with someone in a sexual relationship God must be the highest of all in it. His sovereignty, authority and power must be preeminently fixed in all you do and say.

His truth must take first place in all actions of your life.

Any **violation** of this position will short-circuit the covenant and render it **NULL AND VOID**. Sinful ways, disobedience to the Word will always, without exception, be seen by God as turning to the left or to the right. We are told to walk a straight and narrow road. When we decide to violate God's Word against fornication we are definitely turning to the right and the left. Deuteronomy 28:14 makes this clear:

"Do not turn aside from any of the commands I give you today, to the right or to the left, following other gods and serving them."

In Psalm 27 we can see a great Theos Covenant of Obedience and Blessing.

"The Lord is my light and my salvation—whom shall I fear? The Lord is the stronghold of my life—of whom shall I be afraid? When evil men advance against me to devour my flesh, when my enemies and my foes attack me, they will stumble and fall. Though an army besiege me, my heart will not fear; though war break out against me, even then will I be confident. One thing I ask of the Lord, this is what I seek: that I many dwell in the house of the Lord all the days of my life, to gaze upon the beauty of the Lord and to seek him in his temple. For in the day of trouble he will keep me safe in his dwelling; he will hide me in the shelter of his tabernacle and set me high upon a rock. Then my head will be exalted above the enemies who surround me; at his tabernacle will I sacrifice with shouts of joy;

I will sing and make music to the Lord. Hear my voice when I call, O Lord; be merciful to me and answer me. My heart says of you, "Seek his face!" Your face, Lord, I will seek. Do not hide your face from me, do not turn your servant away in anger; you have been my helper. Do not reject me or forsake me, O God my Savior. Though my father and mother forsake me, the Lord will receive me. Teach me your way, O Lord; lead me in a straight path because of my oppressors. Do not turn me over to the desire of my foes, for false witnesses rise up against me, breathing out violence. I am still CONFIDENT of this: I will see the goodness of the Lord in the land of the living. Wait for the Lord; be strong and take heart and wait for the Lord."

God must be the highest recognized authority in our relationships with each other. When we allow our flesh or our soul realm to become the highest authority we are on our way to DECEPTION.

With TRANSCENDENCY we must always ask: **Who is in charge here?**

"H" **Hierarchy:** In any covenant there is a headship and a submissive status. In the courting stages the headship is up to the man. It is his responsibility to be a godly leader at all times. Any activity that is unpleasant to God will truly be seen by God as insubordination to HIS TRUTH. Sinful practices by one in a headship position place him at odds with God's providence and truth. Therefore, God will refuse to bless the covenant.

On the other hand, if the one in submission within the hierarchy sins, then God refuses to bless the covenant as well. Why? Because the headship is not attempting to terminate the sinful actions and the covenant is thrown out as null and void, totally ineffective and void with God.

Regardless of how you view your relationships past, present, or future it is only what God's Word says and requires of you that gives in a covenant agreement. You have no blood covenant agreement or godly acceptance if you are in the sin of fornication or adultery! This is one of the reasons marriages end up in divorce courts or on permanent battlegrounds because premarital sex is the common activity within the hierarchy of both parties. We are told clearly and without compromise to FLEE FORNICATION. If you enter the sin of fornication or adultery you have given Satan permission to have your body. Paul states so emphatically that your body is the temple of the Holy Spirit. He proceeds to say that *"...The body is not meant for sexual immorality, but for the Lord, and the Lord for the body"* (1 Corinthians 6:13).

When you refuse to recognize the THEOS of God in hierarchy or leadership and submission, you give your body by your own lustful choice to Satan and absolutely anything is possible in his choice of destruction for your life.

One month after I married I met with the president of the college I graduated from and told him I had made a huge error. The marriage began with a phony altar service. A lie!

Purity or Prison

I had not led my partner in courtship to godliness, and holiness, I had taken advantage of her and used my headship to manipulate and hurt her. We went to the altar to recite vows, invoking God's blessing in total disobedience to the Word of God.

Read, if you will, this example of a typical wedding ceremony.

Pastor's Address to the Guests:

When God wished to describe the beauty and unity and completeness of the Church, when God wished to reveal to mortal understanding the happy estate of His people, He chose to picture a wedding—a **devoted** bridegroom with his **spotless**, glowing bride.

WE WERE IN DECEPTION!

We have gathered to share in the joy of these who have come to join themselves as **God's perfect type of everlasting love.** We have gathered here to wish for them **a union which shall rejoice the heart of God and make His picture true before mankind.**

GOD'S HEART WAS BROKEN BECAUSE OF OUR SIN OF LUSTFUL ACTIONS!

Address to the Parties:

This marriage in which you come to be united is a holy ordinance, instiued by God at creation, honored by Jesus

Christ at the wedding in Cana, and commended by the Holy Spirit as evidenced in the writings of the Apostle Paul.

MY LEADERSHIP HAD COMPROMISED OUR BODIES AND MADE THIS HOLY ORDINANCE, HONORED BY JESUS, COMMENDED BY THE HOLY SPIRIT—NULL AND VOID!

Addressing the Man, the Minister Shall Ask:

Having a full understanding of the privileges and obligations of this **Christian marriage**, will you take this woman to be your wife, **to live together in the holy estate** of matrimony, to love and to cherish as long as you both shall live?

The Man Shall Answer:

I will.

MY LACK OF LEADERSHIP IN THE AREA OF SEXUAL PURITY REMOVED ANY COVENANT OF CHRISTIAN MARRIAGE! THERE WOULD BE NO WAY WE COULD LIVE TOGETHER IN A HOLY ESTATE.

Pronouncement to the Congregation:

Now that you have consented together in holy matrimony and pledged your faith to each other by giving and receiving of a ring, before God and these witnesses—in the name of the father, the Son, and the Holy spirit, I pronounce you man and wife.

Purity or Prison

What therefore God has joined let no man put asunder.

OUR ACTIONS OF LUST MADE IT IMPOSSIBLE FOR GOD TO PUT US TOGETHER!

Benediction:

May this holy union ever be **a perfect type of God's great love.** May it be **blessed and used that many souls shall find their places in the spotless Bride of Christ. Amen.**

(Emil A. Balliet; Taken from Minister's Manual II; Gospel Publishing House, Springfield, MO: 1965; Eighth Printing, 1991.)

FORNICATION OR ADULTERY WILL NEVER, EVER, SET THE STANDARD OR SHOW THE WORLD GOD'S GREAT LOVE. NEITHER WILL IT WIN ONE SOUL TO CHRIST IN TRUE CONVERSION.

As I sat with the president of the college and told him of my sin and shame in this marriage I finally felt the sting of sin. The marriage ended in divorce after twenty-one years. Those precursor nine months of lustful moments negated all potential precepts hidden divinely within a godly covenant.

As I think about the twenty-one years of frustration, arguments, and unhappy marriage conditions it is like millions of flashbulbs going off in my mind. Every act of lust before marriage and adulteries after marriage had taken a picture of FAILURE! We had just chosen to ignore God's divine principles and to think we were going to be blessed.

If you are involved in the sin of fornication or adultery at this very moment, this book is your prophetic warning. Turn immediately, repent and seek God with your whole heart. God is not going to let your lifestyle be hidden much longer! The **consequences** of sin will hurt, the **pain** will make you regret all the pleasure and the **destruction** to lives will be the biggest regret of your life!

TURN NOW WHILE THE LOVE OF JESUS IS BEING OFFERED FREELY TO YOU.

With HIERARCHY we must always ask: **To whom do I report?**

"E" Ethics: For a covenant to have validity it must have some terms of agreement. Certain behavior patterns are to be adopted by both parties. What one party cannot bring to the table of agreement, the other one does. Godly commitment by both parties is paramount within the agreement of this ethic. How can a man make a term of agreement with a woman to keep "Theos" (God) in the relationship? He can commit to love unconditionally and in a protective manner. He can commit never to attempt to take advantage of her physically, emotionally or spiritually. You would never allow yourselves to be put in a situation that would allow you to entertain misconduct.

The truth of the matter is that as a man I seek after a wife because God said, *"It is not good for the man to be alone. I will make a helper suitable for him"* (Genesis 2:18).

Solomon exhorts us in Proverbs, chapter 18, verse 22, *"He who finds a wife finds what is good and receives favor from the Lord."*

Peter so aptly states, *"Husbands, in the same way be considerate as you live with your wives, and treat them with respect as the weaker partner and as heirs with you of the gracious gift of life, so that nothing will hinder your prayers"* (1 Peter 3:7).

A woman is a precious vessel who is an heir together with you for your future. If a man learns to treat a woman with such godly principles, God alone assures us that our prayers cannot and will not be hindered.

Within the agreements of a covenant is a hidden ethics clause that states how the man treats a lady while courting her is the precursor, seed sowing, and fruit producing style of the relationship. Only purity, respect and obedience to God's Word will let you live with a holy covenant of marriage. This assures me of His richest blessings when marriage arrives. There is no doubt that a man who will violate godly ethics in a premarital covenant will deceive his wife once married.

With ETHICS we must always ask: What are all the rules?

" O" OATH: The oath is where the blood cutting takes place. When God promised father Abraham that he would be the father of many nations, in chapter 17 of Genesis, a blood cutting had to take place.

The circumcision became the formal part of the finalizing of that oath. I have come to believe that in my next marriage there is a definite possibility of my wife not being a virgin. There are two things I am believing for, one is that a new hymen could be supernaturally regrown within her and two, that as we take communion before we enjoy each other sexually that the blood of Jesus will place His blessing on us as a seed sown into our marriage. In both cases effective blood cutting would exist. Praise the Lord. This belief is for all.

With OATH we must always ask: What happens if I obey or disobey the covenant?

"S" SUCCESSIVE NATURE: The forming of

a godly covenant must have divine purpose of eternal succession. Marriages that begin with premarital sex have the worst of all odds against them. But more importantly, when the very "T" of the Transcendent God is not there the covenant cannot have a successive nature.

Once more, please note that if any one of the above five letters are out of order or if you cannot say yes to each one as to being obvious in the relationship, then it is not a covenant to stand on nor will it withstand the storms of life. God is a Creator of order and never changes!

With SUCCESSIVE NATURE we must always ask: Does this outfit have a future?
If your answer is no to any one of these questions, the THEOS of life is violated.

5 FORNICATION: DECEPTION AT ITS WORST

Upon arriving at El Reno prison my cell mate happened to be PTL's Jim Bakker. For many hours over days he walked with me, gently sharing how prison would become a healing balm to my soul if I would allow God's hand to work within me. It was truly a divine appointment and one for which I will forever be grateful. God knows just how much you can bear.

This prison wilderness had filled me with intensive pain and sorrow. Godly counsel and friendship were the lifelines God tossed out to me while I worked to unravel the tangled mess my life had become. Somewhere in my life I believed a lie and I had to discover how this course of failure came about in my marriage and life.

Satan is a liar. Satan is a counterfeiter. Everything God has for you to bless you, Satan will duplicate with devious intent TO DECEIVE YOU INTO BELIEVING IT IS GOD'S BLESSING.

Anything done apart from total obedience to God's Word is deception and sin. It will lead you to death. Satan's greatest deception and destroying work is when he deceives a man to give up HIS VIRGINITY.

Purity or Prison

She was a missionary's daughter and had moved from Zaire to South Africa. At that time I was helping to direct a youth group in the church I was involved in. She was a beautiful virgin and I got to know her from church and we became good friends. I was supposed to be a godly young man who would protect her. Over the pursuing months our mutual affection began to develop into intimacy of the flesh. Soon our passionate kissing opened an atmosphere of petting with the logical conclusion of sexual intimacy. All the while we practiced our Christian walk in church (hypocricy) and afterward we preferred our flesh and pursued to satisfy our lust-filled and diseased souls.

This went on for about eighteen months. All the time we were professing Christ, working in the kingdom and living in complete deception to fornication. I was given the opportunity to further my education in the United States and decided to take it. We had every intention of being together in the future. She would come to the United States and we would eventually get married. These were our plans, based on DECEPTION!

It didn't take long before I knew my committment to this young lady was non-existent. I met another woman who I married and my actions broke the spirit and heart of the young woman back home waiting for me. She never recoved from this broken relationship and spent years going from one man to another looking, she told me years later, for me.

My life, like hers, was on a treadmill going nowhere but into an alternative lifestyle that eventually led to a destruction I could have never forseen.

Years later I was prompted by the Holy Spirit to seek her out to apologize and ask for forgiveness not only from her, but her family and father also. God is His marvelous grace extended great forgiveness to me. This forgiveness cleansed my heart in a way that will forever be etched in my mind, but still, the price everyone paid for the sin of fornication was a heavy one!

I learned that Jesus promises us IMMORTALITY, but if we take the "T" or the cross out of IMMORTALITY, we end up with IMMORALITY!

Jesus talks about a YOKE in Matthew 11:28-30:
"Come unto me, all ye that labor and are heavy laden, (overworked) and I will give you rest. Take my yoke upon you and learn of me; for I am meek and lowly in heart; and ye shall find rest unto your souls. For my yoke is easy, and my burden is light."

Now Satan comes along with his yoke and it is just the opposite of what we desire in life. Isaiah states it so well in chapter 58 verse 6:

"Is not this the kind of fasting I have chosen: to loose the chains of injustice and untie the cords of the yoke, to set the oppressed free and break every yoke?"

Notice, Jesus talks about His yoke being easy and His burden light, but Isaiah states so precisely Satan's yoke is filled with bands of wickedness, burdens are heavy and the one who is carrying this yoke is oppressed and in need of it being broken.

Purity or Prison

Picture a person with a yoke resting on their shoulders. From there hang burdens attached to bands tied to the yoke. Each band represents many forms of lust of the flesh, lust of the eyes and pride of life. The yoke is of utmost importance for it is the precursor to the strongholds that wrap themselves around you like bands with heavy burdens.

Over the years there is no doubt that the yoke used by Satan over me was one of intense rebellion. The sinful lifestyle I chose to lead was the bands of wickedness, but the yoke was rebellion because I had made a choice to disobey the laws of God.

Psalm 78:8,18 reflect the subtle choice I had made.

" ...a stubborn and rebellious generation, whose hearts were not loyal to God, whose spirits were not faithful to him...They willfully put God to the test...".

For many years I lived rebelliously because I would not live in obedience to God's Word. It became easy for me to go to church, enjoy and be inspired by a provocative sermon and then leave unrepentant. I could openly and secretly lie about my business affairs and adulterous lifestyle yet sit in church two or three times a week and never change.

God desires His Word to convict our spirits and produce a repentant soul.

The Prophet Samuel had to scold King Saul when he said, *"To obey is better than sacrifice"* (1 Samuel 15:22).

Bruce Hunter

David tells us in Psalm 51:17, *"The sacrifices of God are a broken spirit; a broken and contrite heart, O God, you will not despise."*

If you are living a lie, a fornicating and adulterous lifestyle, you are in a seared conscience. Rebellion is obviously paramount in your life! You cannot rationalize it. God says it is so and it is. How could I attend church each week, then go home and continue in my unholy and perverted lifestyle? The minute you enter into premarital or adulterous relationships, displeasing God, that YOKE OF REBELLION attaches over your neck. The bands of wickedness, lies, pride, lust and robbery then wrap around you with heavy weights of DECEPTION and PERVERSION. This is the reason FEAR GRIPS YOUR HEART—IT IS A WARNING SIGN!

You believe the person you are in immoral sexual relations with is the perfect match—DECEPTION! You are not having a love affair, you are in a **SIN** affair and it will lead to brokenness, pain, sorrow and quite possibly physical death. Your **Sin** affair will never, ever be God's will for your life. **It is abhorred by God.** Satan is stealing years from your life, happiness for a future and every blessing God has waiting for you.

You are caught in the double-minded man philosophy James talks about in the Bible. You are unable to live with God in an intimate relationship because you are double-minded and full of false thinking. After my wife divorced me my life ran from one lady to another. I hurt so badly deep within. Remorse, sorrow, rejection and desire filled me.

I tried to immerse it with memories of the past marriage. I tried to immerse it with the pursuit of other activities. But that yoke of rebellion had bands tightly twisted ever so satanically around me and the weights were unbearably heavy. The stronghold of rebellion had to be broken because the state I was living in was pure torture of the spirit, soul and flesh.

God heard my disparaging cry. Through the help of godly mentors I recognized the evil intent of Satan and the YOKE OF REBELLION which came upon me through the choice of fornication and adultery. Over time I dealt with the repentance of these sins and God in His mercy put a wonderful book, _Why The Hymen_, into my hands. It became a reinforcement to seeing how covenant relationships cannot exist when fornication exists. James tells us that temptations lead us to lust and lust to sin and when the sin is conceived then death will result.

My relationships brought more temptations, lusts and open rebellion toward God. Judgment or death were the only options I had left with a holy God. These are your only options too. These unholy alliances will die either through judgment or death. **PRISON AT TIMES SEEMED WORSE THAN DEATH. LISTEN TO ME, TURN AND SEVER THESE RELATIONSHIPS. REPENT NOW BEFORE IT IS TOO LATE.**

Fornication and adultery bring one into open lack of fear of God. In Proverbs 8:13 it states clearly what the "fear of the Lord" is: *"To fear the Lord is to hate evil; I hate pride and arrogance, evil behavior and perverse speech."*

God hates the sins of fornication and adultery! When sinful behavior between courting couples takes place Peter says you fashion your lives after evil ways then lust leads you to ignorance.

"Therefore, prepare your minds for action; be self-controlled; set your hope fully on the grace to be given you when Jesus Christ is revealed. As obedient children, do not conform to the evil desires you had when you lived in ignorance. But just as he who called you is holy, so be holy in all you do; for it is written: 'Be holy, because I am holy'" (1 Peter 1:13-16).

This might be a hard statement for you to accept, but it is truth—*"A man who remains stiff-necked after many rebukes will suddenly be destroyed—without remedy"* (Proverbs 29:1).

There are many walking around in the body of Christ who are "spiritual beasts." If for one sound moment you would allow God to remove double-mindedness you would truly see what God sees. **Fornication and adultery are repulsive to Him.** He offers unconditional love in repentance. As a man, if you are in sexual sin you are robbing a woman of emotional stability, and right standing with God. Her eternal destiny is in your hands. **It is your responsibility to maintain a holy relationship!**

Sexual immorality allows Satan to sell us out and pours us down the drain of life into the sewers of sin. I hope and pray by now you are asking yourself, "How do I get out of this MESS?" TO REMOVE REBELLION WILL DEMAND REPENTANCE.

Purity or Prison

Rebellion started early in my life and has acted as a filter through which all my many life's decisions were made. This deception filter will affect every relationship in your life too. God sent Satan tumbling out of heaven for rebellion. Rebellion is worse than the sin against God's holiness. Rebellion is open insubordination and when it is conceived it brings sin and death. But open obedience towards God brings life.

The way out is **REPENTANCE** and **OBEDIENCE**.

His FORGIVENESS is complete and his LOVE is UNCONDITIONAL.

Today, you have a choice to make to heed the warnings or go blindly into the SIN affair of destruction to the spirit, soul, and body. Prison is not always the bars of iron and the restriction of movement. Sometimes prison is complete abandonment of restriction! The pain, sorrow and suffering will ultimately be the same, however. The choice is all yours.

6 UNDERSTANDING

There is no doubt that the ultimate desire of a spiritual Christian is to be able to walk in God's presence each and every minute of the day. Yet, we all know that this is not done by the swish of a wand or imaginary thoughts, but by a deep inner desire and determination to love, know, obey and do what God commands. Let the Holy Spirit guide you into becoming aware of how a walk with God can be accomplished by an effectual, intimate and progressive understanding of God's Word. God is LOVE and He is also the Father of the entire universe. This universe must have leadership and God chooses to establish it as a KINGDOM. A kingdom is always sovereign in that it is led by RULERSHIP, AUTHORITY and POWER. Each of these are ways in which God governs the kingdom and within it you and I are His subjects. Without subjects, sons and daughters, there is no kingdom and thus no sovereign reign.

God has ordained us to have rulership, authority and power over the earth. The best way I can describe these and how they interrelate is to share a story of my childhood. On a little church mission in the northern borders of South Africa there is a church building. This building operates as a school for the African children during the week and for church services on the weekend. Just outside the church is a small, unsophisticated bell tower. This bell is used habitually to call people to attend church or school. Its sounds are heard for miles around. There is one thing about this bell that needs further clarification.

Purity or Prison

It must have a rope attached so that when it is pulled, the bell will sway from side to side and ultimately cause the knocker inside to hit the sides and send out a beautiful resonating sound. Without the rope that bell, its tower and all the footings are in vain. With a weak rope, tattered and worn, there is always the chance it will snap and leave the remaining piece out of the reach of the bell ringer.

I believe that God's sovereign will is administered in a similar way. Pull on the rope of His Word continually and you will activate His mercies and blessings. Stop being attached to the rope of His Word and doing what it requires and the sound of the bell is hauntingly silent.

Living in God's presence is impossible unless we become chained, inseparably entwined and empowered by the ROPE of HIS WORD! In Psalm 119:105 it says "Your word is a lamp to my feet." In the days of old a lamp containing a candle or oil wick was made to attach to the ankles of the traveler at night. The light spread its rays of light only within a few feet of the traveler. It did not light up the path for miles ahead, nor the paths of others. In Psalm 119:130 we see how God's Word is a light that gives understanding to the simple.

The Bible is very clear about sexual immorality. If we choose to ignore the rope, the ringer in our heart is silent and the sound of silence on God's part and ours is deafening. You become ALONE and VULNERABLE, even though your flesh might be enjoying sin. This pleasure is only going to last FOR A SEASON! Let me give you an illustration of this alone feeling.

I believe God allowed me to experience this so I could plead with you now in this book to turn from sexual immorality, or any sin that is keeping the bell of instruction from ringing in your life.

The day came in El Reno when Jim Bakker was called in the early hours of the morning to be moved to Jessup, Georgia. I will never forget that fateful morning. I felt immense pain as I had come to take on a comfort zone in this prison with Jim at my side to teach and lead me.

My journey to El Reno had come through such sorrowful and painful steps. The Justice Department transported me through a four-state area fully shackled riding in cars, vans and jets. The nights in solitary cells came with such apprehension and sorrow I felt physically ill for two months being moved from prison to prison. The physical and soul stripping became a norm and many nights I lay curled in a fetal position crying out to God for His grace and mercy. When those ominous bars or thick metal doors would close with such resounding clangs of resoluteness my heart would begin to cry out in anguish—you never knew what those dark hellish hours would bring.

Jim left with his warm smile and compassionate disposition deeply imbedded in my memory. How could God do that to me? It was as though the abandonment of family and friends was not enough. Why was God taking the man helping me to make it through each tragic minute of this hopeless situation?

Purity or Prison

The reality of loneliness began to set in like those black, dark clouds on the horizon sending a message of tornadoes and thunderstorms coming to turn everything into a disaster zone. Along with the uncertainty of prison came those weekends when no one would come to visit. The Fridays arrived and by three o'clock I was walking the prison grounds a broken, crying man. Not only had Satan become like a large python by luring me into his grasp, but he had twisted his body around me and was now squeezing every ounce of life out of me. In my imagination I could see this large snake-like devil preparing to break every bone, then with one venomous gulp swallow me up and soon excrete me onto the dunghill of life—wasted and ruined with no purpose.

If you do not pull the rope of God's Word and activate the ringing and call to repentance in your heart, what I went through for years will be nothing in comparison to hell and eternity!

Until you have entered that place of absolute loneliness and sense the world has walked away in utter and reckless abandonment, it is impossible to describe the loss. There was one obvious observation on my part as the days became weeks and the weeks months. Satan loved to see me lonely, but God desired to translate and transform each fleeting moment into a time ALONE with Him, His Son and His Spirit.

I believe that the experience of being alone was a way to feel and experience to some small degree what separation from God feels like. **I can tell you with full assurance, it is not something you want to experience for eternity!**

Bruce Hunter

My brief time of loneliness makes it perfectly clear to me that I wanted to take hold of that rope of the Word and ring the bell to sound the alarm warning men, women and children everywhere. Serving God, obeying His Word and a daily walk of prayer and submission are the ways to stay in contact and not lose the fellowship of Almighty God. I experienced this abandonment in the natural realm and it was almost unbearable. I can't imagine what total separation from God in the Spirit would be like. Please turn from your sins now before it is too late!

I have grabbed hold of the rope of warning and I am pulling with all the strength within me to move the knocker of your heart to conviction and repentance so you will never have to experience the separation of God in your life.

In Luke 14:15-24 we have Jesus teaching about The Parable of the Great Banquet.

"When one of those at the table with him heard this, he said to Jesus, 'Blessed is the man who will eat at the feast in the kingdom of God.' Jesus replied: 'A certain man was preparing a great banquet and invited many guests. At the time of the banquet he sent his servant to tell those who had been invited, "Come, for everything is now ready." But they all alike began to make excuses. The first said, 'I have just bought a field, and I must go and see it. Please excuse me.' Another said, ' I have just bought five yoke of oxen, and I'm on my way to try them out. Please excuse me.' Still another said, 'I just got married, so I can't come.' The servant came back and reported this to his master.

Purity or Prison

Then the owner of the house became angry and ordered his servant, 'Go out quickly into the streets and alleys of the town and bring in the poor, the crippled, the blind and the lame.' 'Sir,' the servant said, 'what you ordered has been done, but there is still room.' Then the master told his servant, 'Go out to roads and country lanes and make them come in, so that my house will be full. I tell you, not one of those men who were invited will get a taste of my banquet.' "

In prison, I had come to realize that my life as a missionary's son had been a table set with wonderful things from the Lord. Like the people in the parable I had no time, as I grew, to partake of the goodness of God. I wanted what MY HAND could provide. I wanted it MY WAY. Now I had reaped the consequences and I wondered would I ever have the invitation extended to me again. In the time of loneliness I began to recognize how truly poor, maimed and blind I had really become. **I had accepted the gutter instead of the banquet hall of bountiful, godly blessings.** When I came to my senses in prison I grieved over the terrible loss of Christ in my life. I repented and cried out with all my heart and He heard me. He sent out the laborers like Jim Bakker and they compelled me to come to the banqueting table again. This time I ran to the presence of God and joyfully anticipated what He had prepared especially for me.

It is through this chapter that I now compel you to come in. We are living in perilous times. We are living in a time when God is not winking at sin any longer. We are living in a time when He is calling out His prophets to give stern, hard and truthful warnings to all that repentance is imperative NOW!

Don't wait to be broken, separated, taken captive and then left broken, bruised and crying out for the "mountains to fall upon you"!

Confess your sins and be restored in the love of God. The cost of letting go of this rope of warning will be great in your life. God is calling you to the banqueting table right now. Don't let anything stop you from receiving the invitation to come into His presence as His bequest! If you think you can ignore the warnings and that your sins will not be exposed you are **DECEIVED**.

When your sins are exposed the shock strips away everything in your life. This exposure is devastating. The becoming nothing is unexplainable. It leaves one feeling worthless, undesirable and wasted forever. Apathy after the shock of exposure begins to settle in. You are so totally stripped of all dignity it brings you to a place of giving up. There is no fight left in you. To stand for what is right at this stage is almost impossible—if self-preservation is your goal. This is a dangerous place to be in. This apathy can decide your destiny forever if you still fail to acknowledge your sins.

Denial will separate you from God! Being sensitive to an inner conviction right now and repentant confession will start you on the road to recovery. You will then enter a place of INTROSPECTION. Here is where God helps you to recall memories of the past regardless of the hurt and the healing process begins. Even though the absolute humiliation of your sins being brought out to the light feels like a living hell, confession and allowing God to search your heart will bring the greatest peace one could ever experience.

Purity or Prison

Denial at this stage can cost you everything.

I implore you while you are privately reading this book to make things right with God. It is not an accident that this book has been placed into your hands. God is still ringing your bell, are you hearing the call to come? Right now, if as you are reading, you feel the conviction of the Holy Spirit don't wait another second. Take the time to ask for forgiveness wherever you are. If you do not know Jesus you need to accept Him as your Savior. He will become the substitution for your sins and the pay the penalty of those sins. The Bible tells us in Romans 10:9,11, ***"That if you confess with your mouth, "Jesus is Lord," and believe in your heart that God raised him from the dead, you will be saved. For it is with your heart that you believe and are justified, and it is with your mouth that you confess and are saved. As the Scripture says, "Anyone who trusts in him will never be put to shame."***

Take a moment to think about what God has placed into your hands. Think about the sins or sexual immorality you might feel trapped in and realize these words and the Word of God throughout these pages has been prepared just for you! Please make the decision to repent, turn and pray. God will meet you with complete forgiveness.

If you have never prayed or don't think you know how to pray, here is a prayer you can offer up to the Lord and I know He will hear and answer.

Dear Lord,
I am a sinner and I have greatly sinned against a holy God and my lifestyle and thoughts have been reproachful to you and others.

I want to be free from the sin and the bondage I feel to it. I want others freed from my selfish actions and I release them in forgiveness right now. I need the precious blood of Jesus applied over my life. I understand in order to have that powerful blood of forgiveness I must accept Jesus as the Son of God and as my Lord and Savior. I accept Jesus now and ask for the mercy and grace of God to reach out to me through Jesus Christ my Lord and Savior. I accept the fact that Your blood can cleanse me, deliver me and set me free to live a life holy and acceptable to You. I ask that others will have it in their heart to forgive me also and not hold anything against me so that Your love may reach them and set them free also. I ask for the Holy Spirit to come and comfort me, encourage me and teach me your ways. I thank You for all things in my life now, because I believe you will only allow what you want for me in my life. I will be a witness for Your Son, Jesus Christ. I will make Jesus my Lord and Savior. I thank You, accept You and the forgiveness You are offering me today.

Name: _____ Date:_____

Praise the Lord, your name has also been written in the Lamb's Book of Life!

Not long after Jim Bakker left, God in His mercy and grace sent a volunteer chaplain into the prison. Jim Green was a retired Baptist pastor/missionary who had gone back to Baylor to become a psychologist. He and I bonded in just a couple of hours. Jim and I became like a father and son duo. I made a commitment to him to subject myself to his mentoring. To this day Jim still mentors me.

Purity or Prison

There is a **DNA** to our relationship. He does the **D**-Discipling, **N**-Nurturing, and I am the **A**-Accountable to change.

Along with another divine placement in my life, Dr. Cottle, I began the process to study to show myself approved. I studied for a double master's degree in theology and divinity. The men God had put in my life truly have had an impact on me. I thank my God in remembrance of them often.

Once I was able to come to grips with my surroundings in El Reno, I chose to see this time as God's pathway to spiritual maturity. For in this time I truly committed to make prison my *oasis in the desert*—like Moses, King David, Paul and others from the past. No, it was not going to be a time to make me BITTER I had decided,and was determined to be made BETTER! I would take the lemons of my life and make lemonade. You see, it is not what the fruit looks like when hanging on a tree that lets us know the taste. When it is squeezed the true sweetness or bitterness reveals it identity—good or bad.

If you have lime in your heart then once squeezed a bitter taste will emanate. If your life has the fragrance and flower of a Georgia peach, ripe and about to be picked, the world will taste God's glorious sweetness and enjoy Him to the fullest. Only you can decide how to take adversity, trials and persecution. Too often, our circumstances tend to lead us into bitterness and we never stop sinning because of an immunity in our thinking that Jesus is not really ready to come and take us home to Heaven. That is wrong thinking. Why? Christ is already here.

Bruce Hunter

Paul says, **"I have been crucified with Christ and I no longer live, but Christ lives in me. The life I live in the body, I live by faith in the Son of God, who loved me and gave himself for me. I do not set aside the grace of God..."**(Galatians 2:20,21).

Prison life had rocked me enough to get out of this immune thinking and realize Christ was with me. I had come to the place I needed to know, experience, and believe his presence resided in me. To know that required major changes in my mind, life, and way of thinking. I was at the crossroads of life and the bell was ringing loud and clear for the first time in years. This intersection is where human pride and godly humility meet. Pride will keep one out of God's presence. Pride is the instigator of all rebellion. When rebellion becomes deeply rooted in one's life a yoke is placed inseparably on your soul. Rebellion takes on a stronghold of stubbornness also. Rebellion and stubbornness will lead to a spirit seared and a soul unrepentant. This state is truly damned, whether you believe it or not, to a Satanic Abyss.

This time I was hearing the bell because of the mentors God had given me. They were willing to pull the rope of the Word of God and give out a sound that I could identify. I chose a new road. I chose humbleness towards God. Like, the church and the school bell of my youth in South Africa, I could once again distinguish the sound calling me to come. It was now calling me to school and training in humility. I was taking the path less traveled. I would allow the Lord to examine me, prove me, try my reins and see what truly was in my heart.

"Examine me, O Lord, and prove me; try my reins and my heart" (Psalm 26:2).

VISION BY PURITY
BY
OSWALD CHAMBERS

"Blessed are the pure in heart: for they shall see God" (Matthew 5:8).

Purity is not innocence; it is much more. Purity is the outcome of sustained spiritual sympathy with God. We have to grow in purity. The life with God may be right and the purity remain unsullied, and yet every now and again the bloom on the outside may be sullied. God does not shield us from this possibility, because in this way we realize the necessity of maintaining the vision by personal purity. If the spiritual bloom of our life with God is getting impaired in the tiniest degree, we must leave off everything and get it put right. Remember that vision depends on character...the pure in heart see God.

7 ASLEEP
AND IMPRISONED

In October, 1992, I was startled by a statement my ex-spouse shared as we once again pursued one of our many confrontations. She emphatically stated that I had become a *business-holic*. This statement infuriated me. Inside of me I could think of all the reasons why she was wrong. Little did I realize she was only touching the very tip of an enormous iceberg of emotional dysfunction and sinful entrenchment which had taken place over thirty years of my life. Only when I was arrested and ultimately placed permanently, I thought, in prison did this statement of my condition begin to make sense.

Living in denial is one thing, but to walk through life totally immune to spiritual reality and with a comatose soul is quite another. Gross immunity to actual sinful living is stupidity at its best and apostasy at its worst. I had truly become a spiritual schizophrenic—Doctor Jeckl and Mr. Hyde. Jim Green, my mentor, along with some others began to gently and with confidence prod me into recognizing the reality of my soul's condition.

As I began to study God's word some of the heroes of the faith appeared to have debased backgrounds also. Yes, God had truly taken some from being cantankerously, raucous sinners and translated and transformed them into heroes of His kingdom. Two men in the New Testament landed in prison and in the book of Acts their stay was well documented. The only problem was that Paul (along with Silas) were resolving their imprisonment in totally different ways than Peter.

Purity or Prison

Paul and his fellow choir member were rejoicing and praising God after having been falsely accused of leading a soothsayer to Christ—to the absolute dismay of her capitalistic masters. They were not only released when the prison shook, but all their fellow inmates, and the senior guard's family turned to Jesus and were baptized. Their spiritual condition at the time was one of alertness and discernment.

As I studied the story of Peter in prison, chapter 12 of Acts, I realized not one of the inmates nor the guards accepted Christ as Savior and Lord upon Peter's release. Why did this great preacher who led thousands to Jesus not even win one to Christ in this prison time? I believe the Lord has given me an unusual insight to this question based on my personal prison experience.

The circumstance for Peter's imprisonment was right after Herod killed the Apostle James with a sword. Peter became his next targeted victim. So, Peter lands in prison, guarded by sixteen men behind two sets of sentinels and one highly secured gate. To understand Peter's frame of mind we have to look at the emotional side of his incarceration.

Professor Victor Frankl, a leading psychiatrist, shares how he and many prisoners of the holocaust went through four stages while imprisoned by the Nazis. I experienced the very same stages of psychological warfare when imprisoned—**shock, apathy, introspection and having visions of release for a future life.** Here we see Peter obviously in a state of apathy.

You and I would act likewise if one of our best friends had just been killed with the sword.

When I finally settled into El Reno prison I found myself numb and only wanting to sleep. The shock of being disrobed in every area of my life had taken its toll on me. Acts 12:6 tells that Peter was asleep at night chained between two guards and behind gates of steel. That was the very night that Herod was to kill him. I believe my eyes would have been wide open and my heart beating too fast to rest. Knowing Peter's personality of wanting to take charge and manipulate his way out of things there is no doubt sleep would have been the last thing on the agenda. Once when I was first imprisoned, friends will confirm, I was working to raise $10,000 to hire another attorney to appeal my sentence and get me out!

Self-preservation would dictate that Peter should have been awake. But shock is a precursor to apathy that will shut one down even during the times of impending death at the hands of a despotic ruler. As I have studied the release of Peter from prison and applied such to my life I have found there are three distinct steps that become necessary for complete and total deliverance. You must read this carefully and with God revealing the truth to your spirit, soul and flesh. If you can apply these very principles into your life, you will soar into victorious liberty with Christ as your liberator. Peter had a church or a group of people outside that prison PRAYING WITHOUT CEASING AND MAKING SUPPLICATION FOR HIM.

I likewise had some that were not willing to give up on me.

Purity or Prison

They refused to let the enemy have victory over my life. I know my father and stepmother were in Canada kneeling before God's throne each and every day seeking grace and mercy for their lost son. Prayer truly is not a last resort, but is the only thing to resort to when a loved one is lost in the muck and mire of a sinful life. The church prayed Peter through. They prayed unceasingly. In the Greek this refers to a condition when an anchor is thrown overboard and settles into the sand and refuses to be moved so the ship will stand fast. What a marvelous thrill to know that like Peter I also had people concerned enough about the well-being of my spirit, soul and flesh to pray for me unceasingly.

When I look at the story in the Bible about Jesus showing up at the tomb of Lazarus there are some interesting similarities in that story to mine.

Jesus and His followers arrived at the grave site in sorrow. Jesus even wept and groaned before He got there. But two amazing things happened for us to look at. Jesus commanded the family and friends to remove the stone from the front of the grave. That was needed to give Lazarus physical exit from the tomb. Then Jesus had them unwind the graveclothes. This unwinding was indicative of the dysfunctions being removed from my life one at a time. Lazarus had to come out and meet his intercessors.

I know that my prayerful friends and family helped remove the stone and the graveclothes of my life.Thank God for loyal supporters who unconditionally nurtured my reconciliation and restoration to righteousness.

Without so many of them undoubtedly my life would have ended in hatred, revenge, self-pity and accusatory fingers directed toward my malefactors.

As you read this book and realize you are in prison to sin you might be wondering who would possibly be praying for you so you might be released also.

At the writing of this book my friends, churches, pastors, and many more are making commitments to pray for everyone who reads this book. So, right now there are people praying for you just as they did for Lazarus, Peter and me.

There are three basic steps for release I would like to cover with you.

STEP 1
You Must Remain Spiritually Alert

Apathy led Peter into a deep slumber. God never slumbers nor does He sleep. His messenger entered that dark, dingy dungeon with godly light. In Acts 12:7 the angel smote Peter on the side and even grabbed and raised him up with words sent from God. Peter was told, "Arise up quickly!" What commanding words. When the angel of God came to deliver Peter, like He does for you and me, it is always accompanied by the word of truth and His magnificent light. Jesus was truth incarnate, life and light. He came into our lives because of the cross. Another interesting factor is that this very same light and powerful word of resurrection to Peter was never seen or heard by his captors.

Purity or Prison

Divine revelation and light from above given to you or me is Spirit-oriented. It is usually unseen and unknown to most around. Stop trying to get others to act on a commanding light and life of God's truth that is for YOUR immediate activation. Others will be deaf and blind to it at that time, since it is for YOU to HEAR and OBEY.

Many of you reading this book have already had enough light put on your situations and personal circumstances that all you need to do at this point is confess sin and obey God with all of your heart.

You feel the Holy Spirit talking to you personally through this book. The fact you are feeling the desire to be released should let you understand the power and the effective purpose of all those praying for you right now.

Not only was Peter to act immediately, like you and me, but speed was of the utmost importance. Obedience never permits delayed action on one's part. Disobedience never permits advancement in godly purposes for one's life. Disobedience is stubborn rebellion and blatantly open mutiny in God's sight preventing His release of grace into your life. Obey that tug on your heart, listen to the words that have already been spoken to you to give you a new beginning and a new life. Don't put off the heart's call to you right now, because if you respond for the good God is keeping you spiritually alert to His answer for you and your situation.

When I study the life of Abraham it is interesting to me that his very first sacrifice was at Mount Bethel. This sacrifice was to secure godly presence in his life.

A dedication of Abraham's life to receive the presence of the Lord into his situation was no different than it was for Peter in that dungeon or for you and me today. When I see how Peter had to go past the first ward, human sentinels, that to me is having to actuate alertness within himself of his spiritual senses. Without spiritual change that brings harmony with God, nothing will or can bring deliverance to you. I had to make a commitment to bring my whole spiritual manhood into line with God. In those initial stages of comatose apathy at El Reno, through prayer, I was awakened to my pitiful condition and made a decision to go God's way from then on. **It was right there at that place of decision I knew I would be free.**

The Apostle Paul says in 1Timothy 2:9 that we are called to a holy walk according to God's purpose accompanied with divine grace given in and through Christ. Peter is called on to rise up quickly. Watch how godly purpose is always attached to godly grace; with supernatural strength the chains fell off automatically without disrupting the sleep of his Roman captors. Whenever the strongholds of satanic forces are broken it always allows for the entrance of supernatural grace!

Our prayers are releasing that strength to you right now, at the very place you feel helpless. God would never have told the angel to command Peter to arise quickly if the chains were going to remain attached. No, arise quickly because the power of God is going to blow the chains of sin right off you as you turn to Him with your whole heart. God's divinely orchestrated escapes are the making of supernatural provision for you. God never makes mistakes.

Purity or Prison

His sovereign will dots all the I's and crosses all the T's.

The word HEAR in Hebrew means: **LISTEN AND DO IT NOW!** Listen and do or hear and walk it out are handcuffed together like two wrists when a prisoner is moved from location to location. These words are INSEPARABLE: HEAR AND DO! I have been literally shackled in chains around my waist and attached to handcuffs on my wrists and it was impossible to force a release without gaining the attention of the guards. As a matter of fact I could not muster up enough strength to even break a chain. Peter was in a stupor, you might be too.

He did not even utter a word when those chains fell off. That is amazing for he was never short of words and usually was never afraid to go where angels feared to tread. This freedom was definitely God ordained!

When I was living in sin God came with messages and opportunities for me to change. I was so dazed because of the clouds of sin around me it was impossible to see His hand at work. Clouds of sin shield against God's light and directions thereby leaving one imprisoned and totally ignorant of the opportunity for escape from bondage.

Darkness prevents spiritual attentiveness. When godly character reigns supreme in your life it provides a spirit that is razor sharp in conviction and a soul that is quick to repent. After the desire to obey comes into Peter's heart, as it came in mine, and I know will be in yours also, specific instructions were given to start the process of the walk to freedom.

GIRD THYSELF: I believe the angel was telling Peter to get his spirit awakened to the procreative forces of God. It also means a practical side to Peter. He literally had to get up and get himself ready to make the trip out of that prison. He had to mentally, physically and spiritually gird himself.

STEP 2
SOUL AWARENESS

The soul is the decision making center of your life. It has three areas through which beliefs and thoughts must journey—the intellect, emotions and volition (willing to activate what has been thought and felt). The soul is either motivated by the flesh to behave in reactionary ways or it is energized by the Spirit of God through your spirit to respond to holy and pure actions. The angel spoke to Peter about putting shoes on his feet.

BIND ON THY SANDALS: I believe that sandals or shoes represent the preparing to activate the thinking, emotions and will to make the flesh do something. It was not difficult to walk out because the Spirit of God had sent a message through the angel and filled the dungeon with great light. Once your spirit is impacting your soul all obstacles that the soul may try to muster up will be defeated in the spirit world.

These sandals symbolize several spiritual attributes that place one's soul in a position of godly influence. These sandals represent the removing of one from satanic slavery into lordship over circumstances, situations and people. It gives us authority over everything.

It represents a necessary preparation to move in a direction of God's bidding. And it reveals a desire that God wants us to be prepared to be carriers of the Gospel of peace.

Both girding and binding represent what Jesus so forcefully encouraged in Matthew 7:24 about how a wise man or woman who builds their house on a rock is assuredly one who is a hearer and a doer of His Word.

The angel's instructions ended with Peter being obedient. When God calls on us to gird up our minds and prepare to walk He is confirming what the Psalmist says so ably in Psalm15:1,2, Here the question is posed, *"Lord, who shall abide in thy tabernacle? who shall dwell in thy holy hill? He that walketh uprightly (his soul volitionally walks in godly uprightness) and worketh righteousness, and speaketh the truth in his heart."* A true hearer and doer of His Word.

There was another instruction given by the angel to Peter who was still in a stupor.

CAST THY GARMENT ABOUT THEE: When we slumber in satanic ways the enemy, Satan, leaves us unclothed. God wants us to wear a robe of righteousness and a garment of salvation. In Ephesians the Apostle Paul commands us to fight against satanic warfare with spiritual armor. This command is similar for Peter was going to need his spiritual armor to be released from the satanic bondage of Herod that ominously cruel night wherein he was scheduled for beheading.

Spiritual armor had to be wrapped around me and the journey through prison one of being acquainted with each and every piece—loins wrapped in truth, the breastplate, shoes, shield of faith, helmet of salvation and the sword of the Spirit. Not one could be left off. Every one had to be recognized as an essential part of my defense and offense if I was to mount a successful warfare against the wiles of Satan in this prison.

In the life of Abraham a second altar was erected at Mount Mamre. I believe this one was to sacrifice all that the egotistical soul could—his family, finances, dreams and visions all had to line up with godly desires. The soul must come in line with a godly presence in one's spirit.

STEP THREE
PHYSICAL AGILITY

"Follow me," the command without equivocation. The angel was not looking for an answer. Just get your act together and come with me to freedom. Jesus speaks with similar command: **"FOLLOW ME!"** I had to learn that obedience is better than sacrifice. Regardless of the extreme pain while obeying, His words were to be followed with only an "amen." The angel never gave Peter time to become a witness beckoning fellow inmates to come with him. Peter still was stupored enough not to know the difference. That is amazing! Here again we see God only asking for two things—Hear and Obey!

Extradition from sinful bondage leaves you with no other alternative.

Purity or Prison

I have a friend who has lived in sinful ways for over twenty years. She has been imprisoned and the angel of God has come to beckon her to leave the prison of sinfulness. Even the chains, wards and gates are open making it easy for escape to freedom. But, she like so many of us, sits in the comfort zone of this dark cell and can't manage to get up and leave because the new surroundings are unfamiliar. Satan gets us comfortable living like pigs in mud. To change to another way of living in godly purity and holiness is foreign and uncomfortable. Why? **It takes effort, self-discipline and it is not easy.** Easy street becomes a comfort zone. Satan loves it that way. God calls on us to flee from evil, seek after righteousness.

How sad to see so many living within a Christian society unwilling to extract their lives from the barnacle hold of Satan. We would rather live in fornication, adultery, child abuse, marital conflict, alcoholism and so many other sinful ways. The entrenchment in sin seems easier to endure than to obey the godly messengers of light and life sent into our pathways each and every moment of the day. You would think people would want to run to freedom. "Whom the Son sets free is free indeed," and when you know the truth it will set you free. My heart goes out to my friend as she lives in double mindedness chasing holiness on one hand and being tempted by satanic power on the other. Then she finds herself tossed like a wave on the ocean of confusion wondering why she is unstable in all her ways. She is tempted constantly to attach herself to men who want to live fornicating lifestyles and then attempt to cover it with the grace of Jesus' blood.

Bruce Hunter

How deceived carnal Christians become! When a godly man enters the scene, one who is unwilling to compromise in dating and physical romance, it is so foreign to her that she would rather live in disharmony with God attached to physical, carnal affection than to walk in bold purity and holiness. Short-term pleasure takes precedence over long-term eternal purposes inculcated within them by a holy God. Like Peter she believes freedom represents a vision that is evasive and cannot come true.

The angel took Peter past two wards (sentinels). I believe each ward represented his *spirit* and *soul*. When your soul is influenced by the Spirit of truth and the flesh is made subject to God's Word, the flesh will respond accordingly, with obedient submission. In Acts 12:10 it took the supernatural power of God to open the iron gate. I believe that gate represented Peter's flesh having to submit to his spiritually strengthened soul.

His soul was activating his flesh into taking the final step into freedom. Yes, when the doors and gates of your cell of sin are opened, the chains removed and the guards of Satan silenced, the last step is to follow the angel of light into eternal freedom and heavenly bliss.

Abraham had one more altar to go with his flesh. God called on him to sacrifice his son. Here was the man who became the first surrogate father and helped to conceive the illegitimate Ishmael. Then God steps into the lives of Abraham and Sarah and Isaac is born. Sarah laughed when told she would have a child, but God got the last laugh. Now God calls on this patriarch to take his son up to Mount Moriah and literally kill his son on an altar.

Purity or Prison

If it would have been me such a task would have been denied many times. Many dreams and even thinking about it in my soul would have obviously delayed that journey. But like Peter there came a time when Abraham had to walk the talk. He physically had to take his dearest and only son up to an altar out of obedience to the Creator of all the universe.

As he lifted that knife a miracle happened. God saw Abraham's heart of obedience, and graceful provision poured out towards him in the form of a ram stuck in a bush. What provision from above!

How important it was for Peter to physically follow the angel into the *one street* past the two sentinels and that huge seemingly impenetrable gate. **Obedience brought him into freedom.** Likewise, I had to physically take my steps each day into the presence of God when at times I did not desire, to praise Him, pray, memorize the Word, read the Word, study the college course, read books and so many other things. **It was never easy.**

The physical side of me wanted to be like the other inmates and just laze the days and nights away. But the physical steps had to be obeyed as I followed God into the very sanctuary of His presence.

Today, I want to command you by the rulership, authority and power of God vested in me to stand and walk out of the prison of comfortable sin and follow Christ, your Lord, into eternal freedom. The time is short and you must act now.

You may not see tomorrow or for that fact the next few minutes of this day. Satan wants to kill you. John says Satan comes to steal, kill and destroy, but Jesus came to give you life and that more abundantly. Get off your rear end of carnal, satisfying sinfulness. Jesus is your only answer and He will strengthen you to walk in his faith in a holy walk.

Hudson Taylor says it so well: "God's will done in God's ways never lacks in God's supplies." King David states, **"All the paths of the Lord are mercy and truth unto such as keep his covenant and his testimonies"** (Psalm 25:10). *Mercy* is the grace of His providence and *truth* is the purpose of His promises. Truth and mercy intersect always. They cannot be separated. God will never call on you or me to act in certain ways without giving us grace with the provision to accomplish it. Iron gates of hell cannot prevail against God's divine purpose. It is time we begin to attack Satan's kingdom with violence implanted in us by a hungering passion to please God. Satan has power but no authority. Avenge satanic corruption in your life with godly purpose and grace.

The angel walked Peter past the iron gate. God did the same for me and He will do the same for you. In Acts 12:11 the angel took Peter out of the prison and down one street. I believe the one street was out of eye contact of the prison Herod had placed him in prior to the execution. God wants you and me to be taken so far away from the imprisonment of sinful living that we will never return. Peter only noticed his location once the angel had departed. God will never leave you nor forsake you.

Purity or Prison

His Holy Spirit and Son will stand by your side until the very end of this lifetime and into eternity. This book is being sent to you, like the angel of light for Peter, to deliver you out of sinful abuse, disdainful sleep and a satanic hold.

Well, the answer to the original question of why Peter had no convert in this prison sentence is finally here. I went through prison aware of Peter's deliverance. It used to infuriate me when chaplains, volunteer and paid, would beckon inmates to become evangelists and go back into the cells to win the lost. Seldom did they emphasize the necessary stages of release Peter had to go through. All they wanted was for a bunch of emotionally sick men to become doers and teachers. They needed to be hearers and doers. I recall being aware of my soul being so dysfunctional that being a true witness was tough. I sent a letter to all my friends prior to going to prison sharing how it would become a mission field. Within months I had a rude awakening. I realized I was sick, cancer of the soul was riddling my life. I realized becoming a hearer and doer of His truth was the only antidote to becoming reconciled, restored, renewed, whole and ready to reenter society.

Cancer patients should not walk from room to room in a hospital to help heal others, yet alone make others aware of their desperate situations of ill health attacking their lives. How unrealistic to think that one who is finally incarcerated can be so secure in his salvation and wholeness that winning others to Christ is even a possibility. The lifestyle of most Christian inmates is at best carnal and at worst hypocritical.

Yes, you may be a preacher or even a volunteer chaplain reading this book and be angry at me for these observations. Sorry my friend, I have been there and done that. Your words of evangelical fervor are Band-Aids to the reprehensiveness of sinful souls immersed in wicked ways. I used to get alone with God and just weep because I could see the hardship it was to just get my own life in order. Wise men are those who have learned to be hearers and doers.

Jim Green introduced one of the most viable healing tools available, _Search for Significance_ authored by Dr. Robert McGee. This course attracted about six men at each session. Yet, there were about 250 men in our prison. Pretty poor attendance considering those Christian inmates who were slumbering in their cells encased with gambling and pornography. Jim asked his students to memorize one verse a week and over twelve weeks a few sayings that would help us in our beliefs and emotions when stimuli impacted ungodly reactions instead of godly responses. Few of those in attendance would even attempt to memorize.

When Ezra entered Babylonian captivity he covenanted to study the law and do it. It is only when he was released back to Jerusalem that he became a teacher. Jesus states with additional force that when someone fails to do and teach His will he will be called least in His kingdom. Therefore, I like Peter was willing to just be a hearer and a doer as it applied to my own situation so I could become extricated from the strongholds of Satan and the comfort of satanic ways.

Purity or Prison

Please, stop trying to make people become soulwinners when they are still emersed in the darkest dungeons of sinful comfort and their souls have difficulty assessing or discerning the truth. **Let them first become hearers and doers.**

Upon release Peter had to be taken far from the prison that once numbed him into a deep sleep. I was assigned a new probation officer seven months after being released from prison. This man can only be described as one fervent in his calling. I misunderstood his initial attempts to be an angel and lead me into *one street* like that of Peter. He called one day at work and demanded I pack my bags and leave the financial mortgage business immediately. Initially, this request devastated me. I had what seemed a perfectly good source of revenue and now it was slipping through my fingers. I was angry at him and at God.

Recidivism in this country is at an all-time high. Seventy percent of all inmates released from prison will return someday to that fenced or walled lifestyle due to their repetitive criminal activity. My probation officer had followed statistics and knew that I was not to be part of the fateful 70 percent. Prison is a great criminal university!

Over the next couple of months I realized the light of this angel sent from God had given me a place of safety and spiritual understanding. Since then I have begun to learn to live by faith and trust God for His provision. He has implemented the writing of this book because I was forced to trust God for His introduction to godly editors and publishers. I have been allowed to work half days so that the doctorate I began in prison can be completed.

Bruce Hunter

God has been more than a friend to me.

It is so amazing to me that once I became willing to obey God's truth in my spirit the first level (ward) of prison was opened, and I was given another wonderful chance at life. This time I am determined to live it in complete obedience without compromise. When my soul was allowed to be stabilized by the truth imbedded within my spirit, ward two was opened. But it took the truth energizing my soul and flesh to supernaturally open the last gate of strongholds so I could live in freedom removed from federal prison.

Allow the angel of God coming to you through this book to lead you into *one street* so you can live free of Satan's bondage forever. Joshua exhorted his followers prior to his death to decide whom they would serve. I like his choice, **"As for me and my house, we will serve the Lord"** (Joshua 24:15).

The Prophet Joel beckons the nation of Israel to a position of making a decision about their relationship with God Almighty. In so doing he does the same to you and me today to become awakened because there are **"Multitudes, multitudes in the valley of decision for the day of the Lord is near in the valley of decision"** (Joel 3:14). Joel says that the end time is near when the sickle will bring in the final harvest and all the words of teaching, drawing and coaching will soon be silenced. My friend, there is coming a day when the call to run out of your cell of slumbering sin will be over. You will be taken at a moment's notice into eternity and be face to face with God.

Your opportunity to walk free from the bondage of sinful slavery is now. It is a choice for you. You are not reading this book by accident. Will you hear God's final words to you as, **"Well done, good and faithful servant?"**

The angel came to Peter and in obedience Peter followed him to freedom. God sent His angels to me, in the form of godly men and women, and I obeyed the mentoring spoken through them towards me by a holy God.

This chapter has shown you how the stages of imprisonment are able to be thwarted if you will gird up your mind, put on walking shoes, place spiritual warfare garments on and follow obediently the light and life of a sovereign God into eternal freedom. You will not be given too many chances. This may be the very last call to stand up in the resolutely dark prison that has its iron gate closed for you to run to freedom while the gate is supernaturally opened because of your obedience.

Let your words be like those of Paul when he finally came to the end of his journey of standing up for the Gospel of Jesus Christ and his Lord and Master, **"I have fought a good fight, I have finished my course, I have kept the faith"** (2 Timothy 4:7).

WHILE THE WORLD WAITED

A most significant event was taking place while slumbering Peter lay asleep in that dungeon of doom. Secretly meeting behind closed doors was a group of people fervently supplicating in intercession for their beloved apostle.

There is no doubt that prayer should never be the last resort when it comes to claiming one's freedom. As a matter of fact, it should be the most important thing to resort to all the time.

Peter was obviously not aware of the words in Job 42:10. This scripture says that when Job began to pray for others it automatically gained his release from bondage.

But, fortunately for Peter, his followers and co-workers in the Lord were on their knees seeking divine intervention. It stated in Acts 12:5 that the church prayed for him unceasingly. In the Greek that refers to a condition when an anchor is thrown overboard and sinks into the sands below securely mooring the ship disallowing any form of movement. These followers were unwilling to budge in their faith. Their hope for his release was born out a supernatural desire with an expectation that it would occur.

When I look at the story of Jesus approaching the tomb of Lazarus I see some interesting factors influencing the raising of Lazarus from the dead. Jesus went to Lazarus with tears, but more importantly He groaned in the spirit. Then it says He thanked God for hearing His prayer. Once He showed an exalting attitude toward God, instructions were given to the people to do two things: roll away the stone and then unwind the graveclothes from the risen Lazarus.

I firmly believe the stone represented a spiritual victory within the spirit of all in that place—Jesus, the family and Lazarus.

Purity or Prison

The unwinding of the graveclothes illustrated the need to unwind soul dysfunctions so that a healthy life could begin again. Even with the spiritual stone being rolled away still the soulical clothing needed to be loosed. Obviously, both spirit and soul had to be dealt with so that physical agility could be successfully accomplished.

What a thrill to know that Peter, Lazarus and I had something in common. There were people outside of our imprisonment totally dedicated to stand in a place of prayer awaiting victorious deliverance. Their prayers released me from my debauched soul before God and allowed me to be released physically from that federal penitentiary and spiritually from the pit of hell.

Thank God for family, like my father and stepmother, and many others who stood by my side. Many of them had been hurt by my lifestyle, yet they never gave up. Without their prayers undoubtedly my exit from prison would have been filled with revenge, self-pity and accusatory fingers pointed at my malefactors. God placed saints at my side every minute of the way and for that I am humbled and most thankful.What unconditional love when only retribution would have been most appropriate.

God is so good.

Stop trying to get others to act on a commanding light and life of God's truth that is for your immediate activation. Others may be deaf and blind to it at that time for it is for **you to hear and obey**.

8 THOUGHTS ARE SEEDS THAT ULTIMATELY HARVEST A DESTINY

"Plans fail for lack of counsel, but with many advisers they succeed" (Proverbs 15:22).

There are two men who have made statements regarding thoughts and the ultimate destiny that I would like to share with you, Andre Maurois and Charles Swindoll. Their statements have been expanded by me because I believe my personal life experience can expand upon their thoughts.

Pictures sown ultimately harvest thoughts
Thoughts sown ultimately harvest beliefs
Beliefs sown ultimately harvest emotions
Emotions sown ultimately harvest willing actions
Willing actions sown ultimately harvest habits
Habits sown ultimately harvests character
And, character sown ultimately harvest a destiny!

Recently, I attended a service and a friend that I became acquainted with prior to prison and maintained contact with during my prison stay was the guest speaker, Reverend Richard Dortch, the president of PTL and fallen partner with Jim Bakker. He spoke so compassionately to us that night. Afterwards Richard, his wife and I visited for a little while.

Upon saying farewell he gave me several of his books. They truly inspired me for within their pages were common memories that only those who have fallen from grace would clearly align with in one form or another. In his book, _Caring Enough To Help the One You Love,_ there is a chapter on failure. His words could not be forgotten for truly I had struggled with them as well. Let me take a few moments and share what Reverend Dortch had to say: "I know about failure and how I was helped when I stumbled. It is devastating. It is ugly to be a public spectacle, to be laughed at, to be scorned. It is terrible to hide from people and not want to show your face. I know that loss. And I have no one to blame but myself. No problem is more personal than failure. No problem involves more shame. There are so many types of failures, it sometimes appears as if society is one great wasteland littered with the fallen. Failure is one of Satan's greatest weapons. He has used it throughout the centuries to bring down kingdoms. It deeply hurts families and relationships. The pain of failure can split marriages and dissolve partnerships. Satan wants us to stay where we are and not get up. Satan laughs at failure. He feeds on it. It gives him a reason to go on."

As I digested those words it only made me more acutely aware of those early days in El Reno once I began to see the light and life of God. With the reading of this book God began to do surgery on me that would take at least fifty months. He began to operate on my life with divine hands of love. He began to do a work in my life that had gone from pictures or images as a child into thoughts, beliefs, emotions, actions, habits, character and a final destiny in a federal prison.

My life had to make one big 180 degree turn. Ungodly thoughts now had to change into godly truth permeating my soul and physical actions. I have never been a drug addict or an alcoholic, but some of the very life-changing actions they must apply to their life for success had to become mine as well. The only difference was that I had no problem acknowledging God as my supreme Creator. God was not some higher power evasively spoken about. He had sent His Son in the form of man to be bruised, broken and bleed on Calvary just for my life. The suffering of His death at Calvary brought an inner strength not of my own capabilities. Christ left this earth, but left a Comforter in the form of the Holy Spirit to give me power, love, joy, guidance and many other powerful tools to rise from the gutter to the glory of victorious living. With mentoring by Jim Green, Jim Bakker, Paul Roach and Ric Freeman, the accent into victorious living was assured. These men taught me how to utilize the free gift of the Lord of Lords and the King of kings in rulership, authority and power.

This return to living in righteousness, peace and joy was taken on as a daily walk. In the very beginning I determined to take only a few hours at a time. It was difficult, especially when the weekends approached. Other inmates would get visits. I would look out the cell windows as wives, children, family and friends frequently came to see fellow inmates. Those lonely days brought tears of sorrow, remorse, anger and questioning of God and His plan for my life. As I moved from hour to hour into a personal relationship with Jesus the lack of visits took on less importance. The necessity for me was to draw closer to God. This became my priority.

Purity or Prison

Satan used loneliness to try and drive me from God. But, I forged a bonding to God where being alone with Him became a respite from the storms of life.

There is a song I listen to by a Psalmist Cindy Holman. It clearly states how I was able to walk those many minutes and hours in prison and never give up:

"You ask me why there's such peace in my eyes
When the road ahead is filled with confusion
You don't see how I can still carry on
When there seems to be no more solutions
Well, I have a Father that I can rely on
He knows my needs before I do
There may be an ocean that stands in my way
But my Father will make a way through.

So if I'm walking on water
Or if I'm marching through the sea
It's the delight of being His daughter
That makes it all worthwhile to me
And that's the difference that you see.

You ask me how I can still wear a smile
When the world seems to crumble around me
You see the pressure, the fight and the strain
And you wonder that I'm still standing
But I've found the secret to living beyond
All the circumstances, all the frenzy
My eyes are on Jesus, He lifts me above
Even though the storm rages about me.

And at the end of the journey

Bruce Hunter

I'll find my greatest reward
To see my heavenly Father
Oh, to be with my Lord.
He makes it all worthwhile to me
And that's the difference you see.

The journey to living a godly life took on a multifaceted form of precepts that had to become habits within my life each and every waking moment. The very sinful lifestyle of the past had to be expunged once and for all. Only God could make the difference. When Satan comes with darkness and death, God brings light and life. I wanted godliness to reign supreme in my life. There are seven basic precepts I try to apply in my life each day.

1. Love God
2. Fear God
3. Know and Obey God
4. Trust God
5. Praise/Pray to God
6. Accountable to Godly Mentors
7. Have Self-Control

These seven precepts were practiced in some way each and every day. I discovered that my life had to slow down. Microwave, westernization in my thoughts and actions had to become subservient to God's ways. If I was to change dramatically and leave prison a godly man, these precepts had to be imbedded in my life like blood coursing through my arteries and veins. These were to become the very white blood cells bringing an immunity toward sinful ways and defending off satanic temptations and attacks.

If you will adapt each one of these to your life beginning early in the morning miraculous changes will occur.

You will become the very image of Jesus and the reconciling force within you will draw all men to God. There is no chronological order to these other than the first three. Yet, all seven were intermingled at all times as an antidotal measure bringing a healthy lifestyle even behind those cruel fences of incarceration. You may not be imprisoned physically, but are encompassed within your soul and spirit with destructive satanic forces. If you make the effort to apply each one of these consistently to your life you will see change.

LOVE GOD

It was one of those days when God and I were arguing about love and hate. Sometime in the first few months at El Reno I was walking the track dealing with a God of love and I was so full of anger. It was difficult. Somewhere in my childhood I had failed to receive the necessary portions of love that made me feel like I belonged, was worthy and competent. As a result I feared failure, feared rejection, felt full of blame and at this point shame flooded my life. Then God spoke a few words that shook me up: "You hated your wife." That was impossible. I refused to accept it. How could I? Look how I provided for her, took her places and enjoyed some wonderful times, the list of defensiveness grew. Then the words of God spoke to me:

"Turn you at my reproof (chastening): behold, I will pour out my spirit unto you, I will make known my words unto you" (Proverbs 1:23).

God wanted me to begin a process so needed in my life. Godly love had been missing from my life for many years. As a matter of fact, I did not understand godly love. Then the words of the wisest man, King Solomon were shared with me as I contemplated how I could have possibly hated my wife. **"Burning lips and a wicked heart are like potsherd covered with silver dross. He that hateth dissembleth with his lips, and layeth up deceit within him; when he speaketh fair, believe him not: for there are seven abominations in his heart. A lying tongue hateth those that are afflicted by it; and a flattering mouth worketh ruin"** (Proverbs 26: 23-25, 28).

Yes, I had lied and attempted to deceive her so often no one could keep count. Lies incubated live scorpions within my heart. They had permeated all other areas of life; business, church, etc. I had to know what the seven abominations were quoted in Proverb 26:25 in order to better understand God's reprimand about how I hated my wife. I had to take a look at the seven abominations and how they applied to my life if I was going to get anywhere with God in my life.

PROUD LOOK
I had truly become filled with pride. I was now in a situation that was knocking it out of me day by day. Each day waking up to a prison cell was quickly showing me the pride that had brought me to this place.

LYING TONGUE
Only I knew too well how the salesmanship ability God had given me had blended with lies and hypocrisy.

HANDS THAT SHED INNOCENT BLOOD
I had not murdered in the flesh, but I knew in my heart my thoughts had gone down this road many times. My tongue got me in all kinds of trouble. The Bible says that life and death are in the power of the tongue. My tongue had slain many.

DECEPTIVE IMAGINATIONS OF THE HEART
Only someone who is bound in their mind can really understand the torment of deceptive imaginations. Pornography, vain thoughts, jealousy, hatred are but a few of the deceptions that gripped my heart. I was cancerous with this level of deception.

FEET RUNNING TO DO MISCHIEF
This was an area I worked hard to keep ahead of others in self-serving ways.

FALSE WITNESS SPEAKING LIES
My character and the lifestyle I was living made this shoe fit a little too comfortably. I even hate to acknowledge this side of my life. It is my hope this book along with the blood of Jesus, are the redeeming factors to correct this great wrong.

SOWING DISCORD AMONG THE SAINTS
I was a master of this. I had become a professional manipulator especially with my wife and especially when she did not fall into my way of thinking. I could create great discord, hurt and sorrow—all to get my way. As I began to look more intently in introspection God began to show me from that day forward the most important commandments in the Bible had to be followed.

Bruce Hunter

I truly did hate my ex-spouse and God because I was not in obedience to His Word. I hated myself and others also. Initially, I would only admit to one affair. I had been on a business trip in South Africa when it took place. That affair made me a carrier of chalmydia, a sexually transmitted disease. God began to deal with me and I eventually was forced into the place where I had to confess and openly admit that there were many others. Nothing can express to you the hurt, sorrow, pain, and frustration my family had to endure because of my selfish and sin-filled life.

Sexually permissive lifestyles outside of a godly marriage or a sexually permissive single lifestyle brings a whorish relationship into union with God and becomes a perversion in the union with God and your partner.

I truly needed to follow the words of Jesus in Mark 12:30 and 31: **"And thou shalt love the Lord thy God with all thy heart, and with all thy soul, and with all thy mind, and with all thy strength: this is the first commandment. And the second is like, namely this, Thou shalt love thy neighbour as thyself. There is none other commandment greater than these."**

Conviction within my spirit brought me to my knees. Out of my soul a repentance was birthed that will live with me forever. The words of God are spoken so vividly. God saves me when my spirit is convicted, but truly draws nearer to me when I repent.

Purity or Prison

David says it is Psalms 51:17 convicted spirit and a repentant heart (soul) make up the holy form of sacrifice that God desires.

Within a few hours a letter was mailed to my ex-spouse repenting for having lived such a wicked and perverse lifestyle. The letter became the beginning of many as I wrote to countless others asking them to forgive me for sinful acts against them. I was experiencing the source of God's love for the first time in my life—forgiveness!

"Beloved, let us love one another: for love is of God; and every one that loveth is born of God, and knoweth God. he that loveth not knoweth not God; for God is love" (1 John 4:7,8).

If you are reading this book and have at anytime been wounded by my sinful acts, with God's help please accept my humblest apology for how I may have wronged you. I am truly repentant for having hurt you and your family. Please receive this from a man who seeks total reconciliation with you through the blood of Jesus.

The precursor to a godly lifestyle is to come to grips with the thought life you may be involved in and the actions you have already done. Then you must begin to accept the forgiveness and love of God. Without it there is no eternal change available to you within the sin-filled darkness of your heart.

This love is so incredible it wipes out the past as if it never existed and God looks at you as a pure, clean vessel. That is a love and a joy unspeakable and full of glory!

FEAR GOD

Satan attempted to fill me with his fear. Prison is fertile soil for this type of fear. Guards and inmates alike will breed, fertilize and bring torrential typhoons of fear into one's life. Satanic fear is:

F   **False**

E   **Evidence**

A   **Appears**

R   **Real**

The fear that Satan attempts to place as a shroud over your life will not materialize in 99 percent of the cases if you cast it down as a vain imagination and only bring godly thoughts into the obedience of Jesus Christ. Satan desires his fear to destroy godly thinking and lifestyle from the throne room of your heart.

King Solomon says in Proverbs 8:13 that the " **The fear of the Lord is to hate evil: pride, and arrogancy, and the evil way, and the forward mouth, do I hate.**"

My hatred of the past had to change. I had to make a godly decision to begin to hate the devil and all his deceptive ways and turn my love towards God. I could not let the spirit of fear get a stronghold in my life.

GODLY FEAR IS:

F	Godly Feelings and beliefs
E	that Energize and
A	Activate a
R	Response toward God.

This responsiveness hates evil and exalts God, the Creator of the universe with a heart filled with praise, obedience, love, trust and a desire to know Him.

A fear of God will create a desire to obey Him. Obedience will bring greater intimacy with God. The fear of the Lord has many attributes. The following verses bring a few to the forefront:

a. Godly Confidence: **"In the fear of the Lord is strong confidence: and his children shall have a place of refuge"** (Proverbs 14:26).

b. Fountain of Life: **"The fear of the Lord is a fountain of life, to depart from the snares of death"** (Proverbs 14:27).

c. God's Bountiful Supply: **"Oh how great is thy goodness, which thou has laid up for them that fear thee"** (Psalm 31:19).

d. Godly Companions: **"I am a companion of all them that fear thee"** (Psalm 119:63).

As I studied God's word on FEAR I noticed that it is the very beginning of obtaining all knowledge and wisdom.

Without fearing God's divine knowledge and wisdom I knew I would never change. **"The fear of the Lord is the beginning of knowledge: but fools despise wisdom and instruction...The fear of the Lord is the beginning of wisdom: and the knowledge of the holy is understanding"** (Proverbs 1:7 and 9:10).

KNOW GOD

I had struggled my entire life trying to determine the will of God in daily decisions. Differentiating between knowledge, wisdom and spiritual understanding was impossible. As I took hundreds of hours in quality time of God's Word it became a lamp unto my feet and a light unto my path. This is the first area you must turn to when you turn away from sin and turn to God. The Bible must become the source book for all of your future decisions and contentment.

I desired to walk in the light of God's countenance. My spirit and soul began to drink from the fountain of His light. Prison was having a refining effect on me because of the unbearable situation I found myself in, but the Word of God was changing me and creating in me a healthy mind like I had never known. As I began to study the Word, and memorize it, a cleansing began in my mind and heart. The entrance of the Word of God in my life began to reveal the innermost darkness within me. There were things I didn't want to admit, but the Word kept shining in like a spotlight and I couldn't miss seeing and understanding my need for repentance and forgiveness in those hidden parts. The word of God became a mirror to my life, daily. I began to hear and obey it. Now, real change and peace were mine for the keeping.

TRUST
"They that know thy name will put their trust in thee: for thou Lord, hast not forsaken them that seek thee" (Psalm 9:10).

Learning to trust God became a very real test of character for me. For too many years my trust was in MY abilities and the efforts of those encircling me. Now, I was living within the rulership, authority and power of the Federal Bureau of Prisons. This kind of induced authority will destroy all human trust in mankind eventually. People were failing me, I was failing myself, and most of all, there was no place or person in this den of evil where a man could find one minute of peace. No, I had to find a trust, peace and place and I did in turning from the world and all it had gotten me to a living Savior who walked with me daily!

Inmates live constantly with change leaving all of them with emotional upheavals. At times fires are set in the trash baskets in the bathrooms just to emphasize their anger. Trust is nonexistent in prison. I was trapped in a system of punishment for my sins.

If you are in sin you are actually in the same system. You might not have had the one experience yet that will bring you into the reality of it. You just have not had to wake up to the restrictions surrounding you yet. Those restrictions are there and sooner or later you will experience them if you don't make a conscious and serious change in your life. One day in the middle of all this misery I read a verse that changed my life.

Bruce Hunter

"It is better to trust in the Lord than to put confidence in man. It is better to trust in the Lord than to put confidence in princes" (Psalm 118:8,9).

Over the years trust in man had failed me time and time again. It had filled me with fear of failure, fear of rejection, blame and shame. Now, I had come to a place in my life where I had to put my trust in something other than myself, I failed, and others, failed to respond to my need, so I began to feel, why not trust God?

Trusting God in your life must become a place where you throw all caution to the wind and recklessly abandon selfish preservation. For a period of twenty months I never got to see my two younger children, Trent and Shauna. Obviously, prison separates, destroys and ravages family relationships. Your prison, without the bars I was facing daily, is just as destructive to your family relationships. I wonder how many of you have really SEEN your children today?

Prison became a time where I had to turn all trust for their well-being over to God. There was no way I could be a father to them while in prison. Men, if you are living in secret or open sexual sin, lies, or a deceptive lifestyle of any kind, you might be bringing a paycheck home, but like myself in prison, you are unable to protect and care for your children. You are not there for them and I guarantee you, they are experiencing your absence every night when you come home! You may be there physically, but your heart and soul are somewhere else.

In the fall of 1996 I received a letter from Trent, my son.

He shared that there were three universities that were recruiting him. I wrote him a letter sharing the benefits and disadvantages of each one. There was one in Tulsa I desired the most for two reasons. Firstly, it would be more closely related to our faith. Secondly, I would be released in Tulsa and truly believed he and I needed a lot of healing. Within a few short weeks his mother wrote back and basically told me to get out of his life. He needed independence and couldn't I live elsewhere than Tulsa.

Trusting God became my only hope each and every day I existed. I began to praise God in this situation for I knew only God could provide the answer.Today Trent is a student at Oral Roberts University and I live in Tulsa. When trust is founded on godly principles, He will never fail us!

PRAISE AND PRAYER

"But let all those that put their trust in thee rejoice: let them ever shout for joy, because thou defendest them: let them also that love thy name be joyful in thee" (Psalm 5:11).

I had to learn to apply praise-filled prayers in my daily life. So often my life was persecuted and the usual and customary tribulation of prison could have sunk my faith. In those early hours of the morning until the late nights I practiced praising God. Praise and worship will be like surgery on your heart. Through praise God will change the convicted spirit and repentant heart into a new heart and a right spirit before Him. I found that praise in my life prepared me to hear God's Word. I made praise a habit each and every day in prison.

Now, I still continue this practice because I have gleaned so much of God through it.

GODLY MENTORING

The desire to become a Promise Keeper father to my children nurtured a deep inner desire for reconciliation, restoration, renewal and wholeness with God. The mentors God sent me began to apply a spiritual and soulish DNA to my life.

D **Discipling**: They began to provide teachings and printed materials that would draw me closer to godly living.

N **Nurturing**: They took valuable time out of their busy schedules to frequently visit me and take many phone calls when I needed someone to lean on.

A **Accountability**: This was needed as they kept watching to see if I would apply their mentoring. The materials they gave me were consumed immediately into my heart. The counsel they gave was applied and never discarded as frivolous. I wanted to clone my life to men who had godly precepts deeply engrained within their walk with the Master.

These mentors began to love me and encourage me, help me set reasonable goals, participate in my needed recovery. They lived unselfishly so I could grow and mature during the most difficult wilderness experiences of my life.

Purity or Prison

To this very day I maintain a weekly accountablitiy to Jim Green, my close friend and mentor. I don't believe that will ever change for he and I have a bonding that transcends all other agendas. If you do not have a mentor take this book as the first step. Share it with someone you respect and after they have read it glean from them. Ask them to be in your life for accountability and mentoring.

GODLY SELF-CONTROL

Once these main points were deeply planted in my life the fruit of such began to show in the form of self-control. King Solomon says in Proverbs 25:28, **"He that hath no rule over his own spirit is like a city that is broken down, and without walls."** For too many years I acted out of impulse driven by false beliefs and unstable emotions. Prison has a way of making you succumb to either hidden anger because you lose all rights to control your destiny or prison can mature one into allowing God to lead. His word must become the source of influence.

Over time God began to work within me. He gave me the ability to see any harmful activating events or stimuli and allowed godliness to prevail within all my actions. Self-control had to become a norm rather than an unusual event. Self-control is the exercising of inner stength that is directed by sound judgment so that everything I think, believe, feel and act out will be pleasing to God.

Inner strength is the ability to moderate my desires and appetites within a holy stance. Sound judgment is the ability to understand good from evil and also to recognize what is good, better or best in regard to God's will for my life.

Jim Green gave me a wonderful book to read. You should buy it today and consume it immediately with a compulsion to learn from it: *Self Talk* by David Stoop. As I read this book it gave me immense insight into taking a life that was once out of control and making it disciplined each day to walking in the footsteps of Jesus. Self-control is by far one of the most difficult tasks to work through. Each day a step at a time consistently walked out will bring you into godly patterns and habits of self-control

Taking time to truly recognize each stimuli or activating event and how it related to my own thoughts and beliefs became a necessity. Repetitive, harmful past reactions were becoming less practiced. They were being replaced by godly responses because discipline in this healing process became my goal.

The first act of discipline you can do for yourself right now is admit it if there is sexual sin or any other sin in your life. That act of confession is the giant step to peace, joy, life and true love.

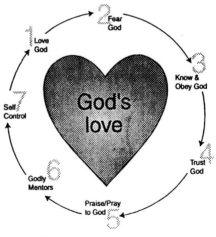

9 THE CROWN JEWEL

You are going to be aggressively tempted to just scan this chapter. I beg of you, do not take the words in the next several pages lightly. The old Hebrew teachers and parents would put their children through a teaching seven times. Somewhere between the very first teaching and number seven the light would go on in the child's mind. The information would become spiritual understanding. The teaching would be elevated higher than knowledge or even wisdom. You may commit right now in your heart to read this chapter, study it, reflect and recollect it up to seven times or as many times as it takes until the light of it shines forth in your innermost being.

The other day a cartoon impacted my life. It was a picture of a very crowded elevator. The doors were just beginning to shut. There was one guest on the elevator who did not belong. A lion had wandered in and its tail was still sticking out the doors. The caption read, "Don't be alarmed, folks. He's completely harmless unless something startles him."

This cartoon carried a great truth behind its humor. The symbolism in the spirit and soul world brings a virtual reality to the ways of satanic prowess. As long as the elevator door remains open the lion's passivity is guaranteed, and the occupants in the elevator unharmed. Shut the door on his tail and watch a vicious rampage erupt and explode into the lives of those within its presence. The Apostle Peter said, "Satan, as a roaring lion, goes about seeking whom he may devour" (1 Peter 5:8).

Vigilance and soberness are always recommended regardless of the fact that Satan lacks authority. Satan has immense power and uses it against those who threaten his domain. As a matter of fact the ammunition Satan uses against you is a direct indication of his fear of you. This chapter will walk you into a lion's den where Satan will try to devour you. Satan hates to see you elevated into the crown jewel of God's presence—A spiritual understanding to lead you into a walk within the perfect will of God.

If you practice the precepts and principles of this chapter, the door of ignorance will be closed that once prevailed in your walk with God. God will lead you into a walk that lacks ignorance and you will live with a boldness and confidence. Additionally, you will become a beacon of hope to those whose walk is where you once trod. The roadway of spiritual carnality and ultimate doom and despair can have the door shut on it permanently. There are three principles you must acknowledge to walk in the will of God.

1. God's Holy Word
The foundation to preserving, guarding, promoting and honoring you as a child of the Most High Father God.

2. Knowledge, Wisdom and Spiritual Understanding
Discernible differences between all three and how they relate to each other in a daily walk of faith.

3. Godly Covenants
How to integrate them into some final questions which will reveal God's will for each and every decision you make.

I would like to ask you to take this time to pray with me about an important aspect of healing, God's Word.

Dear Heavenly Father,
I come to You in the precious name of Your Son, Jesus Christ my Lord. I am about to begin a wonderful journey of being taught some principles that will bring me into such harmony with Your Word. It is so important that Your Holy Spirit teach me these principals so from today forward I can know how to hear You talking to me. My obedience to Your voice will bring me into intimacy with You. It will cement a right standing, peace and joy as I make Your Word the plumb line of everything I believe, feel, do and say. Walking in Your will is my longing. Thank You for clarifying each of these principles Bruce has written under Your authority to bring me Your love, life and light. In the name of Jesus I ask it and believe for it to be manifested in my life.

God's Holy Word
Are you ready to learn something exciting? I am ready, equipped and given a godly authority to lead you into truth. Why? Those who have a godly love to teach help those who have a godly love to learn!

I wish a humorous joke could illustrate this section of truth, but a sobering story will have a greater impact. A young man about to graduate went to many car lots with his father. Tradition in this middle-class family provided a brand new car for graduating from high school. The perfect car was selected, the day of graduation arrived and went without a hitch, crowning the young man with the proverbial cap.

Purity or Prison

At the end of that day of celebration, when all the guest had left the home, the son was alone with his mom and dad. The father sat down next to his son and in his hand was a gift which was presented.

With the highest expectation and emotional anticipation the young man ripped off the wrappings. To his displeasure was a Bible beautifully autographed with his name in gold. In a fit of anger and rage he threw it down on the couch next to his hurt parents and stomped out of the living room. He soon left home and never returned home again. Years later a phone call was received telling this rebellious son about his father's death. The funeral filled him with much sorrow. Later at home the whole family sat in grief around that same living room which had so often been a place of family cheer.

The son went to his dad's desk and opened the drawers to see if there might be something that would bring solace to his grief. There was his Bible. With a saddened heart he lifted it out of the drawer. As he opened the Bible an envelope fell to the carpet. He picked the envelope up and opened it. A cashier's check was enclosed for the exact amount of the price for the car he desired for his graduation present. Hidden for over forty years within the treasure-filled pages of God's Word was a check. Its use was delayed because he misunderstood God's grace hidden within the pages of the inspired Word of God. His failure to search God's Word separated him all those years from his earthly and his heavenly Father.

God has a dominant sovereign will for your life.

Satan is never worried about you until you grab hold of God's Perceptive Will—The holy Word of God written in sixty-six chapters of the Bible! Knowing God's Providential Will never threatens Satan. It only is when you activate God's truth, His Perceptive Will, that Satan begins to shuffle with nervous anticipation. Satan is a serpent, deceptive and sly. He has a plan that I call: **I AM IDLE.**

Here is how it works. It is a staircase descending downward predicting spiritual comfort and lethargy regardless of the pew you sit in each week at church or even the degree of service you render to your parish. You can attend the most anointed services and walk out as an .I.D.L.E. Christian. Satan's plan slyly descends you into the carnal abyss of a spiritual and soulish grave awaiting the shovels of mourners to someday cover you with real dirt when your flesh collapses under the darkness of death.

You will never fully comprehend that will until you know His Perceptive Will (the Word of God) and His Providential Will (grace and mercy from the love of God).

Purity or Prison

Step One: **I Am**—You are fully agreeable and willing to participate. Nothing is forced on you.

Step Two: **Ignorant**—Hosea, the prophet, says that people perish for lack of knowledge or because once they get the knowledge they choose to reject it. Satan wants to steal the Word of God as it will keep us ignorant. Paul, the apostle, says when we do not have the Word, our understanding is darkened which alienates us from the life of God through ignorance. If you stay out of God's Word you will definitely see Satan resting on his laurels.

Step Three: **Deceived**—John, the apostle, while he was banished to the island of Patmos tells us even more of Satan's strategy. Revelation 12:9, reads **"And the greater dragon was cast out, that old serpent, called the Devil...which deceiveth the whole world."** Yes, Satan's deception covers the whole world. Paul says we are blinded in our hearts. Once blinded, deception is easy. Satan is aggressive and ruthless in his deception. God's Word is a road map out of deception.

Step Four: **Lazy**—John, the apostle, calls the church of today a lukewarm bunch. Riches have come as a way to comfort the body. There is nothing wrong with wealth unless it begins to make us lazy in studying and applying God's Word to our life daily.

Step Five: **Entrenched**—This is the final step Satan provides most Christians to rest in absolute apathy. Millions of church attendees, especially men, routinely walk into church while expeditiously committing lascivious acts of sin as a way of life.

Lascivious living! What is that? It is at the entrenchment stage Satan places you in that daily living which eventually results in a total lack of self-control, a casual immunity to sin and a flirtation with ungodly ways. The apostle Paul writes, **"Who being past feelings have given themselves over unto lasciviousness, to work all uncleanness and greediness"** (Ephesians 4:19).

Feelings: Ignorantly deceived toward God's Word leading one's emotions into illegitimate feelings soaked in irrationality.

Given: Feelings providing unrestrained will leading to a perverted lifestyle.

Work: A moving and working with purpose toward the filth of the world earmarked by Satan for those who have taken the I AM IDLE WALK.

God's divine Word is the antidote to the satanic plan. King Solomon shares a divine, supernatural staircase into the presence of God. I call it the **I FLEE** precept. I FLEE from IDLE ways Satan tries to place me in. I choose to step up to godly ways.

Jesus says, **"Ye do err, not knowing the scriptures, knowing the scriptures, nor the power of God."** (Matthew 22:29). He is in concert with King Solomon. His Word brings a powerful light of God's Word into your life, a powerful light of God's Word that cleanses you from sin, a powerful light of God's Word that keeps you from sin and finally a powerful light of God's Word that reveals His eternal pathway for every step you take.

Purity or Prison

King Solomon introduces these steps in an ascending manner in Proverbs 4:6-8. These five steps lead to intimacy with God and knowing His will.

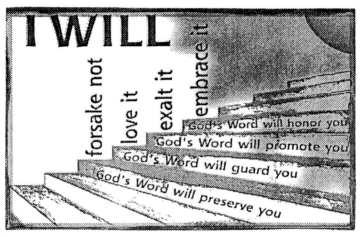

I Will
Only you can decide not to set a place for Satan in your life and choose to make God's Word a priority each day.

Step One: **I Will**—This is where you have to make a conscious effort to FLEE from IDLE ways that Satan wants to keep you entrenched in. You see God's Word as more than an hors d'oeuvre on your table of life. You recognize it as the only way to build an immunity within your soul to the deceptive ways of Satan. **I will** says: "I will become persistent, enduring, perpetual and continuous in daily engrafting God's Word into my life. "

Step Two: **Forsake Not**—Paul speaks about dying to self daily. Self lives to find the easy way. Becoming a person who forsakes idleness is difficult. Why? Years of practice encase one's lifestyle in easy living. To forsake Satan's ways means you will have to run to God's arms.

Prison revealed feelings of being forsaken by those I once loved and cared about. There is a loneliness in being forsaken that cannot be described. God feels forsaken when we snack on His Word. Consuming it is the opposite of forsaking it. God then comes and preserves us as we consume His Word.

In the Hebrew language *preserve* means to take a garden, plow the dirt, spray insecticides on it, seed it, water it, weed out the unwanted, fertilize it and water it over and over again. It brings ultimate harvest when diligently preserved. Forsaking not and preserving go hand in hand. I forsake it not and God promises to preserve me.

Step Three: **Love It**—This is not erotic or soulish in nature. It is the agape love that comes through a spiritual entrance. Then it enters the soul and effectively unwinds in physical actions for all to see and hear. I watch couples courting and they do everything possible to be together. Why? There is an all-consuming love between them. In prison my love for God's Word removed all desire to watch TV, play pool, play cards, read novels, and other things that would have distracted my attention from God's love for me. I learned that His Word was made flesh for me, Jesus. I learned the greatest love ever known to man.

A love for God's Word guarantees He will keep you. The word *keep* really means to guard you. Guard! Only a prisoner can know the true meaning of that word. A guard keeps one away from others who will hurt or maim him. A guard keeps one from escaping into a lifestyle of being wanted. God guards us where we are unable to do so in every situation.

Purity or Prison

God's name is a high tower, we are to run into it and be guarded in safety.

A garden must be guarded from varmints of life. Solomon says when we guard our hearts with God's Word, out of it will come the forces of life. What are those forces? Galatians 5:22 calls them the fruit of the Spirit.

Step Four: **Exalt the Word**—Webster's dictionary states that to exalt means "to place in an eminent position, to dignify and elevate by praise, to magnify and extol." For too many years I depended on my exalted efforts to promote me. My performance appeared to work well at earning the approval of others which in turn earned many promotions. The powers of positive thinking replace the exaltation of God's Word. They in turn earn temporary results. The power of exalting God's Word into a position of permanence each day earns one supernatural exaltation that has eternal purpose. God's Word exalted in me leads His righteousness before me into unequivocally divine purposes.

Step Five: **Embrace the Word**—It is interesting to see how the principle of FLEE begins with forsaking things of the world and not forsaking God's Word. Then it ends with a clinging, embracing, hugging of God's Word. I recall my children hugging onto my legs when times came for me to leave for work or a trip, "Daddy, don't leave." God asks us to do likewise. Webster's dictionary calls it, "to clasp in the arms, a gesture of affection, as a mark of affection or passion." Embracing God's Word is the highest form of intimacy. The result of the embrace is godly honor.

Bruce Hunter

The Hebrew definition of *embrace* is, "to be placed in a position of esteem, glorious greatness, might and wealth of the Almighty God. Idleness with Satan weighs me down with the world's wealth. Fleeing to God's Word and ways elevates me into glorious realms of godly wealth.

I FLEE

Winston Churchill says it so well, "People who are not prepared to do unpopular things and to defy clamor are not fit to be ministers in time of stress."

Fleeing from idleness into the Word is highly unpopular in the world today. Yes, even pastors have such an overwhelming demand for those to serve in the church that little precious time remains to consume the Word of God. So, when the time comes to minister to others in time of need the vessel is empty of His Word. It is truly unpopular to run from Satan's idleness into the all-consuming Word of God. People treat one like a freak if more than ten minutes is devoted to studying the Word of God.

It is my firm belief that the ultimate measurement of your spiritual capabilities and capacities are not based on your genetic talents, spiritual giftings, intellect or advanced forms of education, but are based on your obedience to the Word and the will of God.

10 THE POWER OF CONTENTMENT

In prison I went through a severe trial and ended up in a wheelchair. As time went on I was wheeling around the camp spinning wheels, running red lights, skidding on wet floors, managing to get to eat in the early chow lines and also causing havoc with men's ankles. Yet, within the heart of one man, a guard, was brewing a deep hatred for me. Unknown to me he was stalking with a relentless fervor. At the four o'clock count all inmates are to stand at their bedside. Being unable to do so effectively I had chosen to place my wheelchair just in the doorway of my cell. Having four men to all stand and be counted is quite impossible in such small quarters. For weeks this practice was used. No guard ever complained. Then, out of the blue I was called down to the guards' office and unhappily given an "incident report" by a man who knew me well. The lieutenant was angry with this man and felt he had been inconsiderate, seeing I was still in the wheelchair.

I was shocked as the report stated I had failed to obey orders three times and I also had made it difficult to do a count causing them to make a mistake. The report had been written and the damage had already been done. Now, the only recourse was to just wait it out and allow the administration to do their review and make a decision as to what discipline would be handed down. Within the week I was called into the camp administration office to appear before the committee. Prior to this I had considered calling on senior staff for help, but God had spoken so clearly to me about the verse in Proverbs 21:1.

Purity or Prison

It basically says that the heart of the management was in His hand and He would lead them into the right decision. As they sat there it became obvious after several telephone calls that the guard who had written the report against me was not considered credible. The outcome was an answer to prayer. I was given full and complete exoneration.

This outcome made the guard mad and others along with him. They contended that the administration had not stuck behind him. But, after the camp administrator signed the expunging of the "shot" I was told to be sure my locker was squeaky clean, as the guard would definitely seek revenge. For over forty months I had been in prison and my file was free of any offenses. Every bit of my record shows as excellent attitude. Praise the Lord.

Time would not be on my side regarding this guard. He had my number and he was going to get me, sooner or later. During this time I began to tutor a parenting class with over thirty students. The lady guard who teaches the class placed me in a position to store part of our material for the class in my locker. One night I needed to do some copying, so, I went to the guard's office and spoke to one guard about getting some copies of material that were in my locker. This suspicious guard stood in the office listening to my request. Within thirty minutes I was called up to the office, handcuffed and made to walk across the street to see the lieutenant in the higher security prison. The guard made up his mind and went over his senior officer's position. Now I was going to pay for the administrations' support of me earlier. He was determined to inflict as much damage as possible upon me. Now was his chance.

When in the lieutenant's office I was accused of the worst of inmate crimes: forgery of certain documents and selling the material to be able to buy supplies at the commissary. As I sat there in absolute astonishment, within me Satan began to have a heyday. I was terrified! This would not look good on my record especially since I was within nine months of final release. The guards began to relish the way of revealing their authority. "You are a crook, a criminal, a forger and you are going to the hole right now. Take this man to solitary immediately," demanded the lieutenant.

As those iron handcuffs dug into my wrists, my body swelled with pain and an iron peg stuck out of my foot. I hobbled helplessly with this camp guard firmly grabbing my arm and pulling me along the cold, empty hallways to the infamous hole. The guards booked me in and dressed me in a full orange jumpsuit, then they took me to my cell. This is the last place any inmate wants to go. It is totally poured concrete, little or no windows to see the light of day just a little window in that massive steel door so one can see the hallway outside the cell. A small door opened within this massive door and the guard shouted for me to back up to it and place my hands through so he could remove the shackles. I did, and pain filled my wrists as I did his commands. I was now in my cell. There were men crying, angry, anxious and in revenge filling the air with sounds and words one could never convey. **The door closed with a bang as if to say, "I have you in my jaws and I ain't gonna let you go!"**

The "cell" was cold and sparsely furnished. After all it is a 24-hour lockdown. The same cell is used for murderers and rapists. Coldness gripped my heart.

Purity or Prison

I recalled the first two months of having to go through this when they first incarcerated me. I sat on the bed, it had no sheets. Across from me was a little desk and then over to one side was a stainless steel sink attached to a toilet. HOME! Only God knew for how long. My heart continued to sink. Stories from inmates who had gone through this before and lived to tell about it began to permeate my soul. Some had stayed in this place for months with no resolve to their problem. It is like a morgue for the living. The staff act disinterested once one is put in this place. **It is the abyss of incarceration**. A cockroach walked ever so bravely across the floor in front of me. I could only imagine trying to sleep and having that creature walk across my face. The pain from the recent surgery I had gone through began to get worse. My foot felt like a football, swollen and in much pain.

It was in this lowest hour I heard within me the voice of God assuring me this was not my end. He knew I needed help and it was time I started getting my training in the Word out of the theology closet and hammered out on the anvil of my heart with practical application. The Word was about to be tested in my life. **IT WAS NOW PRACTICE WHAT YOU PREACH TIME!**

One of my fellow inmates was a bull rider. He had earned seven world championships. God started to remind me of this man's victories. He spoke gently to me, yet with confidence about how Carl had not sat on the couch all the time to learn how to be a bull rider. No, Carl had to get on a bull and learn to ride. Being wildly thrown in every direction he held on for dear life.

Bruce Hunter

It was time for me to put into practice what God had been showing me for years, since the first day I was imprisoned.

As I contemplated this there arose within me a force that emphatically said it was time to get up and let the enemy of my soul be scattered. I chose to stand and start singing praises, praises, praises and rejoicing in all things! Over the next few hours His Holy Spirit began to minister to me as I turned to Him for strength. I then began to quote verse upon verse and finally came to a place of contentment. In those few hours I learned a great lesson: **THERE IS GREAT POWER IN CONTENTMENT!**

Holiness, love, faithfulness, humility, contentment and thankfulness are godly traits because they acknowledge and exalt the character of God.

HUMILITY acknowledges God's majesty.

CONTENTMENT acknowledges God's grace and mercy.

THANKFULNESS acknowledges God's goodness.

With all that was going on in my life, why would I add one more difficult task, ANXIETY? Contentment dismisses anxiety and worry because it is the place where one truly recognizes the all-sufficiency of God's supply for one's daily needs (big or small). The all- sufficiency of God's grace and mercy can reach you in every circumstance or situation you may find yourself in regardless of time or space.

Purity of Prison

When you or I fail to live in contentment it is a direct indication of one's dissatisfaction with God's provision! I needed to make some clear decisions in this situation I found myself in.

Would I fear God, live in the light and know God would never leave me, fail me, or forsake me or would I cower dreading every second in this torment fearing the unknown, darkness and loneliness?

I HAD TO MAKE A CONSCIOUS CHOICE AND SO DO YOU!

I had to enter into contentment because the alternative was so bleak.

The Word had to be activated in my life just as it has to be in yours. This was the time I was going to see how this Christianity really worked.

Psalm 23:4 says, **"Yea, though I walk through the valley of the shadow of death, I will fear no evil: for thou art with me; thy rod and thy staff they comfort me."**

There was death all around me in that place. Death of the spirit of man, death of dreams and hopes, death in the physical realm, death to living! I was in the shadow of this death, but contentment in whom I had believed walked me through it. I could see it and hear it, but it could not touch me. The rod and staff of God's Word and prayer were truly comforting me. Contentment was mine as we passed through this shadow land.

Bruce Hunter

Psalm 91:5 says, **"Thou shalt not be afraid for the terror by night; nor for the arrow that flieth by day."**

There is no fear like the terror the night hours could bring in this pit of hell. I was commanded not to be afraid and it took every ounce of my faith to turn from fear and lay my head down to sleep. Contentment came to me like a baby. He caused His beloved to sleep; and I did soundly.

Psalm 147:3 says **"He healeth the broken in heart, and bindeth up their wounds."**

There in that cell I could praise, read, pray, fellowship with God with contentment because my heart was mended and my wounds healed. I imagined the wound Jesus took for me and realized my hurt was on His body. He offered me healing in return. What started as the darkest hours of my life became the contentment of my soul. There is no place so dark and vile that His love cannot reach out and touch. He touched me. Oh, how my God touched me!

Trusting means that you learn to wait with a courage that never quits holding on. In the waiting season you must "LEARN TO WAIT." What God wants in our life is contentment, no matter what the trial and circumstance.

God's bountiful supply of mercy, grace, love, peace, joy and so much more is available for you too. It doesn't matter what you are facing. God will not desert you if you will but trust Him!

He wants godliness with contentment which is great gain!

Purity or Prison

Therefore begin the journey to contentment. Run from anxiety and worry. Live in godly peace. Begin now to fear God, know His presence, trust His Word and rejoice!

There is great power in contentment.

You can only experience this power as you determine to put contentment into practice!

11 THE HIDE AND SEEK OF SECRET HURTS

It was one of those spiritually exciting days in solitary confinement. I had been sequestered there under false charges that were later expunged. As I sat at that small, metal table with hot food in front of me, a marvelous peace flooded my soul. I looked at the food thankfully. I lifted my head to my Father and my prayer soared from a heart that was overflowing with thanksgiving. Even when in the most unlikely of places, there is never a reason to be so full of sorrow it robs your joy. The Apostle Paul knew only too well the storms of prison life; yet, he could always rejoice. Therefore, as I sat humbly before that delicious prison meal, my soul filled with godly truth to rejoice and again I did rejoice!

While eating just the first few bites I heard the Holy Spirit speak to me within my innermost being. The message He was delivering seemed odd to say the least, "Anoint all the corners of this cell and the doorposts as well!"

The command was so startling that I stopped chewing on the food and turned around to see if someone was in the cell talking with me. I knew that God was desirous of my total obedience, but I looked around the cell and became dismayed. As I bowed my head and looked into the food, thoughts gushed from my heart. I have nothing to anoint the cell. Here I was in a cell far from the reality of freedom and seemingly unable to follow through with God's simple command.

Purity or Prison

At once my heart began to question that inner voice. After all, why would someone be expected to obey when the necessary provisions were missing? Yet, I knew God was not kidding, and His command had to be obeyed.

Tears began to course down my face because of the awesomeness of His command and my inability to follow it. I began to cry with a fervor that only an obedient heart can acknowledge. Oh, how I wanted to obey God, but there were no anointing sources within this cell. "Lord, how can I follow through with what You have just asked me to do when no wine or oil is available?" My mouth uttered this prayer in humble meekness. A silence prevailed. My food was forgotten for the moment as the Lord and I meditated on this question. It seemed like ages before He spoke, but one thing I have learned about God is to always trust Him. He will always answer, especially when He has just commanded you do something and the provision to accomplish such is seemingly not there.

"Use your salad dressing. It will represent the blood and oil for divine protection and sealing!"

"Praise God!" I shouted out loud as the tears ran across my lips and almost landed in that orange-red salad dressing. What a marvelous solution to this call for obedience. With absolute urgency I scooped up a teaspoonful of the salad dressing, got up from the folding chair and purposefully moved toward the large, solid-metal cell door. With praise in my heart, the words of Isaiah flowed forth from my lips so loud that Satan and all his imps could hear: "No weapon formed against me shall prosper!

One more time for you, old devil, just in case you're deaf. No weapon formed against me shall prosper!"

With guided holy hands I dabbed a finger full of dressing on the cold metal frame of that doorpost. Persistently, I moved around the cell joyfully placing generous amounts of that salad dressing, now anointing wine and oil, in all the corners of this cell. When I finished anointing the cell I began to recite many of the verses that I had hidden in my heart over the years regarding God's protection against the power of Satan. The blood of Jesus protects and shields against harm. The oil of the Holy Spirit seals it eternally. It reminded me of the children of Israel being instructed by Moses to dip hyssop in blood and paint the doorposts so the angel of death would pass by their homes. I recall James Dobson sharing how he and his wife did that to their home for protection against Satan's attack. If it worked for them, then it would apply to my situation, too.

A quiet peace began to reign supreme in that cell. It is always that way no matter where you are, especially after God's commands have been obeyed. I seated myself and began to eat the rest of the meal. A smile covered my face because I knew there is never a reason to disobey because God will always provide. I recalled God's words to Jeremiah in the first chapter of that wonderful Old Testament book. Anywhere he was sent he was to go, and any words given were to be spoken. I could not help but think of what had just happened to me. Maybe this solitary confinement was becoming a time to beat out God's truth on the anvil of my heart. Just maybe this was a small step of many upcoming giant ones in which God would call me to obey and find me a willing servant.

Purity or Prison

Yes, that was it. If I could prove my trustworthiness to God in the small steps, then He would eventually call me to actions that would have greater significance.

After finishing the meal I settled down to study more of my Master's words. Suddenly, there came this shouting down the central hallway from a man who appeared angry at the world. As the noise got closer, I got up to stick my face against that small cell window to see what all the commotion was about. The guards brought this small-framed, Hispanic man to the cell across from me. As he turned to enter the cell, my eyes caught his and there could be seen hate buried deep within. His shouts became growls as they released his shackles and slammed closed that huge metal door. Triumphantly, the guards walked away, but this man was left screaming; screaming for help that would not and could not come in the form of human means. I realized in that very instant only by the cross of Christ could this man gain eternal freedom.

As this untamed human paced in the cell his voice turned into screeches, growls, barks and inhuman curses! The pitch of his voice raised and lowered as though anything but a human was within his body. I knew what was across from me; Satan had entered this man and possessed him. When I called on the guards to come and help him, they laughingly mocked and replied, "He's praying to his gods!" But I knew his condition and was filled with compassion toward this man who was so full of evil. For the next two days this man stayed awake banging, screaming, shouting and cursing. He would glare at me through his cell window. Only the door held him back from hurting anyone.

I tried to get his attention; with a smile and cupped hands I motioned that I wanted to pray for him, but all to no avail. His cursing and disposition only worsened. Ultimately, a psychiatrist came and prescribed medication that made him sleep.

Then God reminded me of that anointing wine and oil. Wow! Providentially God knew that I would be placed near this demon-possessed man, and that supernatural protection would be needed. Yes, in every situation you and I come in contact with there is potential for demonic danger. God knows way in advance how to prepare for us, the hitch is we must obey to receive the blessing.

As I remained in God's presence those days, the noise and threats from the demon had no effect upon my time alone with God. I was surrounded by angels. The blood and oil of anointing assured me of God's loving and protecting arms. When God is in control, no mad man can attack or bring harmful effects on saints! Praise His holy name!

In looking back on that incident there is a marvelous sense of thanks within me. As an inmate, a convicted felon in the eyes of the world, there is something to learn from this. Both myself and the demon possessed man were in prison for sins we committed. We were both in solitary confinement. The difference was I was not hiding sin and I was seeking God with my whole heart. I had, through confession of my sins and repentance, been placed back into the protective covering of love from my Savior. **I began to realize through my journey of immorality to prison that when HURTS are allowed to remain a SECRET, the ABUSE gains great POWER!**

Purity or Prison

It became more obvious to me that every human being has a power within them guiding each step of the way on that eternal path to somewhere; a godly one that will end in eternal peace or a satanic one that will result in total exclusion from the presence of God and sorrow forever.

Secret hurts come in varying packages. Most of them are incurred while a child growing up in dysfunctional homes. These hurts are allowed to become hidden deep within the soul for many years. These deep, hidden hurts are the result of sexual, physical, emotional and spiritual circumstances that have impacted a person's life consciously or subconsciously. Regardless of the root to the abuse causing the hurt, the facts remain that when one allows them to dwell in the darkest of closets, they incubate dysfunctions. The longer these are kept secret they become all powerful and manipulate your daily living.

Regardless of my location (physically) God was there watching over me in this hellish incident. Why was one so protected and the other given over to demonic powers? The answer lies in this important fact: I had made a conscious decision to turn from my sins and to seek out the dysfunctions of my life through the gentle leading of the Holy Spirit. I wanted to find any hidden hurt and get it on the altar of God. I came to a great truth in those fateful days of a mad man's unquenchable horror. It was simple:

THE BLOOD OF JESUS! IT WAS THE BLOOD OF JESUS AFTER I CONFESSED MY SINS THAT TOOK MY CRIMINAL, SINFUL, LIFESTYLE AND CONVERTED ME INTO A SAINT!

Recall with me the story of the crucifixion. Jesus was between two thieves. One mocked Him and refused to recognize his sins for being there.The other made the statement that he deserved to be on the cross because of his sins, but this man, Jesus, did not deserve to die. He then asked Jesus to remember him when He would go to his Kingdom. The thief was told by Jesus, **"Today you will be with me in paradise"** (Luke 23:43). Two men so close to Jesus, but two so different approaches to His saving grace. Two judgments were passed that day, one to enter into hell and everlasting torment, the other into heaven where there will be no more pain or sorrows. The fact the thief would be in heaven was based on his acknowledgment of his sins and of who Jesus was. He was not keeping them secret and hiding anything from the Lord or man. He had taken the first step in repentance. Acknowledge your sins to God and He is just and faithful always forgiving you and cleansing you.

The famous actor/comedian, W. C. Fields, worked hard all his life and earned vast fortunes. However there lay deep within his inner man a secret hurt that was never dealt with and purged. Over the years he would open a bank account in every town that he performed in. He even got off trains along routes to his next performance and opened an account at the local bank. All his accounts were in anonymous names.

Not until after his death did the estate realize that over 700 accounts had been opened. One was in Germany containing over $50,000! He died without even enjoying the money to the fullest or even allowing those less fortunate to have a small piece of his fortune.

His best friend was asked about this peculiar behavior. In response his friend told them that for years W. C. Fields would awaken with a terrible dream. He would dream that every town he went to he would be broke, without food, poorly dressed and without a place to stay in inclement weather. So, he decided to open an account in as many towns as possible. If ever any of those events actually occurred he would never be without money to meet his needs. Just to think this man of fame and wealth succumbed to such foolish acts of FEAR shows how powerful an influence secret hurts can have in your life.

DENYING EMOTIONS

The effects of hiding secret hurts, or denying emotions, impact people in different ways. Our emotions interpreted into actions reveal the true inner energy that secret hurts mobilize each day to thwart one's maturing. Our dysfunctions have a way of alienating one from building healthy relationships. Instead they cause one to associate with others who have the same hurts and lack of maturing in life's cycle.

Once you make a conscious decision to seek out those places in life where hurt has been hiding you will discover a wonderful way to deal with life and issues in a healthy and peaceful manner. When we add secret sin to secret hurts we are on a collision course with mental, physical and spiritual breakdown, as could be seen from the mad man in El Reno. Anytime secret sins are left unchecked the victim walks through life dysfunctional and unable to truly enjoy a healthy inner peace and satisfaction in life.

These hurts impair one's relationship with God. That impairment can distance one so far from the grace of God that the sinful actions take control and you are in desperate need for deliverance. King David says it so clearly: **"There is no soundness in my flesh because of thine anger; neither is there any rest in my bones because of my sin. For mine iniquities are gone over mine head: as an heavy burden they are too heavy for me"** (Psalm 38:3,4).

God wants us free of these secret hurts and sins. Continuing to harbor them removes us from an intimate relationship with Him. The longer you allow the hurts and sins to stay within the hidden cervices of the heart, they will eventually deaden you to any knowledge of God.

Today, regardless of man's location or condition of the heart, the blood becomes eternal grace, given from the life of Jesus to all who will accept Him as the Son of God. The Psalmist states we are never to forget the wondrous works of God. The blood did not just start at Calvary to atone for sin, it was spilled in Genesis to clothe the sinful nakedness of Adam and Eve. It was spilled in Abraham's era as a sealing of a covenant between him and God. It flowed annually on the day of atonement for the sins of the nation of Israel. But, primarily, it began as sweat drops in the garden of Gethsemane as Jesus began His final steps in that long journey to the cross. As blood poured from His side, down His weakened legs, onto a wooden cross to ultimately soak into the soil below, its significance shattered the rancor of oppressors. A veil in the temple was torn in two, thereby bringing the kingdom of God out of a man-made structure into the heart of believers, you and me.

His blood spilled for you and me and if we confess sin, trust and obey, that same blood ushers us into being joint heirs with Jesus; sonship of God guaranteed. Within me there is a new kingdom reigning.

Yes, I could sit in that solitary cell, which had the anointing of a simple man who believed, "No weapon formed against me can prosper." Like the repentant thief on the cross I had entered a place the other thief and the mad man of El Reno failed to find.

I had made a giant step in understanding!

12 FROM
SCOUNDRELS TO HEROES

"The argument is now put forward that we must never use the atomic bomb until, or unless, it has been used against us first. In other words, you must never fire until you have been shot dead. That seems to me to be a silly thing to say" (WINSTON CHURCHILL).

This may seem an unusual statement to begin this chapter with, but there is a great spiritual truth I wish to share. Why would I utilize Sir Winston Churchill's discussion about the atomic bomb? As an inmate, just before my release, the thought of having to face the world with such a tarnished reputation caused me to consider many things. I knew I had to consider two alternatives. One was to be passive and the other assertive. I believe that God would want me to be assertive. I believe that He wants my reach to exceed my grasp and then allow His grace to empower me to successfully complete each mission He sends me on.

This means I cannot wait for Satan to come and attack me. God wants me to live in the position of power. He wants me to attack with the supernatural omnipotence of His grace. He has given me first strike capabilities. **Spiritually dead Christians cannot attack**. They have a false illusion that they can respond after the bomb. How wrong they are. We have to stay alert, ready and have first strike capability. Regardless of my past, He is my Father and His instructions are for me to enter the battle.

Purity or Prison

Over the past several years since my very first night in prison He has been preparing me with the washing of the Word. On a recent Gaither video I could not resist weeping for Calvin Newton as he asked his Gospel singing family to forgive him for all his past heinous actions. As he talked about prison, empathy rose up within me. Then he sang like a songbird and the listeners, including myself, could only assure him of God's grace. I am one of those "Calvins" along with past bunkmate Jim Bakker, Richard Dortch and others. The rectory has had its leaders defrocked and some are now my good friends. We all have to reenter society.

The eyes of the world are upon us, some with those of grace and others with mocking jaundice. Yet, we cannot cower or refrain from the message implanted deep within us by the call that is without termination. With God as my Father there is too much of His grace extended to me to worry about those who would reject me. His grace is my sufficiency, in my weakness He makes me strong. He can still use me because I have surrendered to His complete lordship in my life.

As I began to study I realized the humanness of all men from several studies I did about men of God from the Bible. These men had lifestyles that showed large inadequacies in their personalities. Yet, as they encountered God those past and present inferiorities were made to look like dwarfs in God's eyes. God never takes the qualified ones to serve Him. He takes those **He can qualify** and places them into His service because of their obedience.

Bruce Hunter

Let's look at Moses:

This man would truly be part of today's "death row." He murdered a man and then hightailed it to Sinai. For forty years he was hiding from those who had him on the Egyptian FBI list of "MOST WANTED." His name means "son of water," drawn forth, and is possibly symbolic of being the one to draw those out of bondage. Psychologists would have made a fortune on this man if counseling him became their daily routine. For in the Word of God it is so obvious that Moses suffered from all the emotional dysfunctions of belonging, worthiness and competency. In layman's language that means he suffered from fear of failure, fear of approval, blame and shame.

There is so much to consider in the life of Moses since the escape from Egypt because of the murder charges levied against him. Here was a man who had spent forty years tending the dumbest of animals. During these herding years, Moses had little known contact with God in the form of theophanies. Loneliness, isolation and separation impacted his life immensely. I know how I struggled with being unable to contact my three young teenagers when first incarcerated and divorced. The inner hurt was at times unbearable, but my pain was to last only eight years and five months. I cannot imagine what Moses went through for forty long years.

Then, out of the blue, or shall I say the wilderness, burns this small shrub. Yet it does not burn up completely. It is supernaturally on fire without the ashes forming. Then God speaks to Moses.

Purity or Prison

I don't know about you, but that would have shocked me, and probably left me feeling totally inadequate. Silence from a God he hardly knew or understood as a child growing up in the palaces of Egypt was now speaking directly to him.

Then over the last forty years beginning to believe in God way out there in that wilderness, he is directed by God to be the deliverer of the Jews. The psychological effects would be diverse, complicated and most difficult for this outcast of Egypt to comprehend. No wonder he had to receive absolute confirmation from God that this mission to deliver three million Jews was real and would end in success.

I struggle this day with the call of God on my life to warn men and women of the terrible consequences of disobedience and sexual immorality. A past sinful life and subsequent separation from society, especially from those I love, has left me with many questions and reservations that Moses must have felt. Even when I feel the Holy Spirit prompting me, I still have to make sure my trust in Christ supersedes my questioning disbelief that God could use someone with a past like me. I have met many inmates and those **imprisoned in the outside world** who must learn to deal with God's desire to use them regardless of their past.

Next, Isaiah.

Here was a man who claimed from his own mouth that he sinned having unclean lips. He even felt that living amongst the heathen had tarnished his life in God.

But God sent a seraph to impart a message to him. Within his hand was a live coal from the altar. That coal came from God. God is a consuming fire. When this fire touches one's life **without the blood of Jesus coating it, there is eternal condemnation.** However, when the fire from God impacts one's life that is propitiated **through Christ's blood, there is eternal commendation.** Praise the Lord!

The seraphim spoke with boldness to Isaiah after having touched his lips with the coal. He was told his iniquity was taken away. There was an immediate apostatizing of sin: all the ill effects were cleansed. He was told his sin was purged. They were fully atoned for because of the blood on the mercy seat. The next step was the seraph asking, **"Whom shall I send?"** (Isaiah 6:8). Isaiah, now washed and cleansed could with all conviction say, **"Here am I; send me!"** (Isaiah 6:8)

The removal of sin and its stain is instantaneously done when the coals of God's fire touch our lives. Isaiah could now move on with the being sent by the One from above.

Isaiah came from the "aristocracy" of the priesthood. He was raised within an environment of sensitivity to sin and being in close contact with those who lived sinfully. When he was called on to be a prophet, all of this caused him to question his ability to be pure for God's message to be carried to kings and others. For this and other reasons, we see Isaiah openly concerned about being tainted by sin. He did not want words to proceed out of his mouth when sin was part of his life. He well understood that as a man thinks, so is he. He also knew that out of the abundance of a man's heart a man speaks.

Isaiah was married and had two children. His name implies "Jehovah saves." We see his writings contained in sixty-six chapters of the Bible. Many theologians have stated that the book of Isaiah should be considered the fifth gospel. It has more prophetic statements about Christ's coming to earth than any other book in the Old Testament. This was possible because when God called him Isaiah believed God. All of this from a man who believed when God called him that he was a man of unclean lips, but was about to experience the cleansing fire of God to be used mightily by Him! He believed a God who chose to see him pure from that moment on in his life.

While in solitary confinement the Lord placed it upon my heart to study how Paul saw himself in light of the cross of Christ. For those of us who have committed sins that have had an immense impact upon those around us and including ourselves, the life of the apostle Paul serves to be a good example for us. Paul uses his energy to expunge the Christian faith once and for all. Senior Pharisees that used him to fulfill their selfish desires also fueled his fervor. Paul was by far the greatest enemy of the Jerusalem church. Stephen's death was a great satisfaction to him and spurned him on to persecution of the church. He had Christians arrested, murdered and imprisoned.

But, as is so wonderfully shown in the book of Acts this apostle was stunned by the brightness of Christ's presence while on a mission to exterminate the followers of the risen Lord. Paul was impacted by that supernatural visit. He became the very opposite of what he originally set out to accomplish. Over the years to come, and until his death, this famous Pharisee would be wanted by his past colleagues.

His message to the world would be received with open hostility. This supernatural encounter is where we see Paul coming to grips with his past lifestyle of debauched persecution and sin against the body of Christ.

As I studied in my infamous solitary cell, shrouded in concrete from top to bottom with no way of escape, my past sins began to haunt me. I wanted to move on, but my mind kept reminding me of the past. I believe the Holy Spirit had me study the life of Paul as a precursor for the Holy Spirit showing me I could be changed forever to the glory of God, too. Paul writes clearly about putting all the past behind him and striving for the prize of the high calling.

Paul's new life was in Christ and Christ was in him. The old had passed away. If I could just make you understand we all struggle with past sins in our soul realm, but it is the power in the forgiving blood of Jesus Christ that gives us a glorious second chance.

Why not turn now from sin and sexual immorality before the cost is so great you cannot hear or call out to the living God like the demon-possessed man in the cell across from me at El Reno?

When one truly grasps the fact of REDEMPTION and how it gains access to God's infinite love, there is a corresponding energizing force that empowers one to live a holy and righteous life. Past lifestyles are over, all buried in the deepest sea and with a "NO FISHING" sign posted right above the mess. Jesus paid the price for all. There are no special blue bloods and other commoners.

Purity or Prison

The redemption of Christ and His blood are the great equalizers. **Jesus paid it all with no discrimination.**

THE NEW LEAF

He came to my desk with quivering lip
The lesson was done.
"Dear Teacher, I want a new leaf," he said.
"I have spoiled this one."
I took the old leaf, stained and blotted,
And gave him a new one, all unspotted,
And into his sad eyes smiled:
"Do better now, My child!"

I went to the throne with a quivering soul
The old year was done.
"Dear Father, hast Thou a new leaf for me?
I have spoiled this one."
He took the old leaf, stained and blotted,
And gave me a new one, all unspotted,
And into my sad heart smiled:
"Do better now, My child!"

Author Unknown

Upon leaving prison, God has given me a new leaf. Through confession and turning away from your sins He has a new leaf for you too. Each step I take, each sermon given, every page written and every word and action will begin to fill this new leaf in my life. It is my desire that when the page is full, it will be said that Christ's image is reflected in me. My prayer is the same for you.

God has a new leaf for you. He will take the old one and place it in the sea of forgetfulness if you will only let Him. Then to the wonderful surprise of us all He has a plan and wants you to reflect His Son Jesus so all the world can see Him clearly. God will lay all of your past, as He has done mine, at the feet of Jesus and then inundate it with the blood of Christ leaving you white as snow.

The choice is up to you: The past? or The future?

13
A LETTER

Shauna, my twenty-two year old daughter, called the other day and made a startling statement,"Dad, I've been thinking recently how bad it was for the Judge in Denver to have sentenced you to such a long sentence. Dad, this justice system is out of hand. Long sentences like you received serve no purpose but to break up families, wreck financial stability on the children and leave the community having to pay for housing, food, clothing and everything else you can think of."

As I contemplated her words, an inner grieving mounted. How could she have come to such an indifferent conclusion? How could she not have seen the change in her father at this point? Then I asked her to wait until the final publishing of this book. I knew within its very covers would be answers to the questions she was asking. Then I entered a time of serious contemplation attempting one more time to clarify in my mind why I needed to remain in prison for fifty months, not thirty, nor even sixty months. God allowed my prison stay for the length of 10 percent of my life. For this I am most thankful to my Father God in heaven.

Submission to Authority—For most of my life a rebellious spirit denied openly any accountability to authority within my life, whether it was to my parents, pastor, employer, the government, or more importantly to my Lord and Savior, Jesus Christ.

Purity or Prison

Upon being sentenced it angered me that the judge stacked the sentences instead of making them concurrent. How could he be so evil?

As I began to study God's Word, a verse kept smacking me across the forehead attempting to gain access to my spirit and soul, **"The king's heart is in the hand of the Lord, as the rivers of water: he turneth it withersoever he will"** (Proverbs 21:1). God was behind the scenes working through figures of authority in my life with divine intent to bring me into a spirit and soul wholeness.

Once placed in prison you can kiss your freedom for release good-bye. Appeals to higher courts for early release fail about 95 percent of the time. God had me just where He desired so change could come. I began to recognize that the justice department was not my captor but God's way of keeping me within a boundary to turn me in His direction through a spirit of conviction and a heart of repentance. Paul states in Philippians 1:6 that God started a work in me during that prison stay that He would be faithful enough to complete. The struggle to fight my way out of prison ceased when I truly saw the light of God's intentions.

The Breaking Process—During the reading of this book three distinct areas have been outlined. In all actuality there are four. Paul says in Philippians 2:5-11 that Jesus went through an immense humbling to come to this earth. He states that the very mind of Christ must also be in you and Me. In other words, what Jesus went through, you and I might have to experience too.

The result of Christ's death and resurrection are stated in verses 9-11, **"Wherefore God also hath highly exalted him, and given him a name which is above every name: That at the name of Jesus every knee should bow, of things in heaven, and things in earth; and things under the earth. And that every tongue shall confess that Jesus Christ is Lord, to the glory of God the Father."**

An important issue must be recognized in the verses above. Tongues will never be able to confess Jesus Christ as Lord until there is an absolute humbling and bowing of the knee, a contrite spirit and a broken heart in total submission to Christ. Prison became the beginning process of many furnace experiences I'm sure I'll experience over my lifetime. Within His furnace a refining is continuing to take place even to this day and will never end until Christ's return. For fifty months I willingly, as painful as it was all the time, allowed God to burn out those impurities.

Yes, I had to go to prison. Yes, I had to be there for fifty months of my life. No, I did not enjoy it and no, I do not ever want to return to prison as an inmate again. God's ways are not my ways. His thoughts and ways are higher than my thoughts and ways. He knew what He had to do in my life to get me to the place of complete surrender. What will it take for you?

As time for my final departure drew near I lacked one last experience. I had never won anyone to Christ while in prison. Yes, I had been very active in chapel and even became a teacher/pastor to many men.

Purity or Prison

At the same time my youngest son, Trent, was graduating from high school in June, 1997, and I wanted to be there. So, I filed a motion that would have given me five months early release. Enough time to get out and be approved to leave the state for his graduation.

Within me a desire to practice what I had studied and walked out was beginning to be a tug I could not shake. At this time I was working in the slaughter house gaining an 800-hour certificate for meat processing and slaughtering. One day a black man, about twenty-eight years old, arrived in prison from Fort Worth. Jay Eubanks came from an influential home. He knew better, but a greed for money, sex and the power of life lured him into white collar crime. He heard that I was well-trained as a white collar criminal. So he attached himself to me. I maintained a stance that my past would not be glorified, only Christ would be spoken of when give the chance. Jay continued to persist to hear how I had swindled so many. But I stood my ground.

Soon he and I were working out together at the weight pile. I was zeroing in on him to accept Christ as Lord. Then all hell broke loose. One day while preparing to cut meat, he and I were fooling around. I grabbed his knife and without thinking he grabbed for it. Instead of the handle his hand grabbed the razor-sharp blade. The blade cut deeply into his hand and instinct did not say loosen the grip bit. He slid his hand off the blade creating more internal damage. Blood squirted all over. Jay fainted. Panic set in. I just about fainted. Twenty-six stitches later and in immense pain Jay and I became ensnared in a battle for our very friendship.

Muslims and others blamed me. A white South African that hates blacks became labeled to my blue prison clothes. I began to pray desperately for a reconciliation, Jay's soul was at stake. God heard my cry and within a few weeks Jay and I began to reconsider the very tactics of Satan; stealing, killing and destroying so Jay would be lost in sin.

Things began to change. His common-law wife was also praying. Then one Sunday Jay went to church with me. The message was a clarion call for repentance from sin. God had sent another messenger to help me bring this lost sheep to Him. Jay never went forward but spoke to me as we left the chapel. He said it was time to meet Jesus and make Him Lord. That afternoon we met out under the trees and God began to bring a catharsis within his life. Today, Jay remains in prison and is actively pursuing God, plays drums in the chapel services and his wife is excited about his release this August. Jay has a call to preach on his life. Please continue to pray for Jay and Shay Eubanks.

Yes, I missed Trent's graduation, but I never missed bringing a lost soul to Calvary. Trent's graduation did not have eternal ramification, but Jay's salvation will surely bring glory to God eternally. Oh, the heart of the king (Judge) is truly in the hand of God!

The day of departure was finally here. I wrote the following letter to friends and relatives a few weeks before I was released. Release from prison is such a time of triumphant expectation. Every inmate awaits the call of his name over the intercom to say it's time to go home to relatives and friends. I believed it would be the finest day of my life.

Purity or Prison

June 6, 1997,
Dear Friends,

"Twenty-five" nights to sleep on this narrow, thin mattress bunk bed and to stand at 4 p.m. every day to be counted as a prisoner. Then to arise early in the morning of July 1 and hear the infamous bellow over the prison intercom: "Hunter, yes you, Bruce Hunter, come to the guard office!" All my earthly belongings permitted to accumulate in this prison, all neatly packed into a small cardboard box, will be hoisted shoulder high and a final farewell to cell mates and others around me. With a brisk and excited cadence, I'll make my way down that Second Street hallway for the last time. Some Christian buddies will meet me for final hugs, joyful tears and a short prayer.

Within minutes a guard will meet me at "R&D" to process paperwork, check my belongings, issue me a pair of jeans, a shirt and boots. Then that final walk out of the brick prison facility into the fresh early morning Oklahoma blue skies. Two large and big rows of razor sharp fence will stare at me as the guard and I approach. They will be the only remaining barrier keeping me from freedom. Freedom from prison chains, handcuffs, walls and fences.

"OPEN THE GATES"

The guard will call over his walkie-talkie to the guard in Tower No1. Soon two huge, heavy metal gates will be electronically released. The guard will open one at a time and I will walk through to freedom. Undoubtedly my face will smile from ear to ear.

Words of "Good-bye and God Bless You" will burst forth from my mouth. Such words of blessing and cheer will surely be drowned out by the finality and definitively resolute noise of the gates closing and the guards simultaneously uttering their farewells.

CLANG...CLANG... The echoes of the gates will bounce off the concrete brick structures behind me. Unlike four years ago, no handcuffs attached to my wrists securely fastened to a chain around my waist nor leg irons assuring limited motion with my feet will hinder my efforts to get to the bus station. Even though the clanging of gates will never be heard again as a prisoner, only one who is incarcerated knows so well that such sounds will from time to time echo through the archives of my soul. For me such sounds will be a constant reminder of past sin and incarceration, but to see God's mercy and grace through it all. This "Prison/Oasis in the desert" will forever leave me with something to praise God over and to know there is no valley too deep for God to lead me through, especially in years to come. Within a few short minutes a Greyhound bus will be transporting me to the Tulsa Halfway House. As I ride down the highway, fifty months of memories will flash through my heart, but longevity of such will be overridden as I learn to cherish the excitement of God's next stage for my life.

I have to believe that the Israelites never forgot those dusty trails and hot days of the wilderness even as they crossed over the dry Jordan riverbed into their "Promised Land." I will cherish this prison experience for eternity.

Purity or Prison

Prison? Yes, prison! This is the very location where I progressed beyond seeing Jesus solely as the Savior of my life. Here is where I made an eternal decision to make Him LORD AND MASTER of all I believe, do and say. Here is where through His Word my life became aligned more closely to the Word that Isaiah said, "Lord, send me." Here is where God's challenge to Jeremiah to go where God sends and speak only what God says became my life commitment as well.

Resident within my heart is an overwhelming awareness that God has a purpose for my life; regardless of my past lifestyle, current imprisonment and any apprehension towards my future, His Word assures me of much.

Within my heart is an ever-growing hunger to know my Lord and please my Father above. Re-entry into society after fifty months of imprisonment will take some challenging adjustments. Needless to say your prayers and intercession will be coveted. Thanks for being my friend over these very important years. God bless you immensely.

Sincerely...A Friend in Christ,
Bruce W. Hunter

Unfortunately, that letter and the expectant jubilation never occurred. I did walk through those clanging gates, the echoes of the closing gates did reverberate off the prison walls and I did say farewell to the pastor and his staff of the church in El Reno at the bus stop. As I seated myself on the bus tears began to fall unceasingly. I truly realized that the calling and gifting was about to be tested.

Within me a voice began to taunt, "Has all this time been a jailhouse religious experience?" I could not get that out of my heart. With just $50 in my pocket and a one-way ticket to Tulsa each mile seemed to take forever and an age.

Was this new adventure into freedom going to be paved with ministry to reconcile souls or, was I a fraud? Then the Holy Spirit reminded me of the passage of scripture given to me December 7, 1995, **"Arise, shine, for your light has come, and the glory of the Lord rises upon you. See, darkness covers the earth and thick darkness is over the peoples, but the Lord rises upon you and his glory appears over you. Nations will come to your light, and kings to the brightness of your dawn. Lift up your eyes and look about you: All assemble and come to you; your sons come from afar, and your daughters are carried on the arm. Then you will look and be radiant, your heart will throb and swell with joy; the wealth on the seas will be brought to you, to you the riches of the nations will come"** (Isaiah 60:1-5).

Yes, on the Pearl Harbor Memorial Day God gave me this passage of scripture and told me it would be the foundation for a future ministry. Then without hesitancy I went to Matthew 12:9-14. Jesus was about to heal the man with the withered hand.

In one sentence revelation knowledge came into my spirit: **"Then saith he to the man, Stretch forth thine hand. And he stretched it forth and it was restored whole, like as the other"** (Matthew 12:13).

Purity or Prison

In these few short words the Holy Spirit revealed that the arm was restored to its original position. Then it said it was whole. It did not need any therapy after all those years of no use. And "it was like the other." It was as healthy and able to work just like the other hand. I was now being released to join all you "healthy" ones to become a reconciler of sinners into the kingdom of God. Wow!

Then God reminded me of Philippians 2:12,13. I truly had worked out my salvation while in prison with fear and trembling. He would now step in and energize within me to will to do of His good pleasure. From that point on a greater sense of confidence filled my life for in it I knew God would not send me anywhere without His righteousness going before me.

I love what Dr. T. L. Osborn says and I paraphrase it, "God created, Satan messed it up, Jesus fixed it up and now I'm back to normal. God now trusts me for He gave me His Word. He chose me and has enabled me. He has sealed me; He deemed Adam, redeemed me and now deems me. He connected me because He put His hand in Christ's who put His hand in mine through the cross and resurrection. God gave me a passion for souls and now I desire to have all mankind know God through Christ."

Recently, my editor shared a short message that stirred me into a deeper awareness and I pray it will do the same for you. It is a story about a preacher who was speaking at the funeral of a church member. As he was trying desperately to say something "nice" about the man, he faced the reality of telling the truth at all cost.

He said, "Today we are burying a church member. What I can say about him is that I never knew him to be a regular attendee. He did come at Christmas and special times of the year, but he was a church member. I don't know of any money he ever gave to meet the needs of the church, people or missions, but he was a church member. I don't know of one person he ever visited to tell about the church or invite them to come, but he was a church member. I don't know of one person here who came to the saving knowledge of Jesus Christ through his witness, but he was a church member. About the only nice thing I can say about the man is, he was a church member."

There is a vast difference between being a member of a church and a sold-out disciple of Jesus Christ. Oswald Chambers says it this way, "The disciple is one who has the new name written all over him; self-interest and pride and self-sufficiency have been completely erased." Disciples are in essence obsessed by the one they follow. Discipleship plants within them a violence to only do one thing carry out the mission of the leader to whom they attach their lives, time and actions.

Who are the men and women who are going to take the kingdom of God and bring it to a lost and dying world?

1. The **IMPORTUNATE ONES:** These are disciples who will persist to shake, rattle and roll down the gates of hell without fear of personal reprisals from Satan. These disciples only fear one—GOD! This fear of God drives them into a hatred of evil and the destructive acts it places upon mankind.

2. The **IMPROBABLE ONES**: These are disciples who have come from the depths of sinful living, like me, and are not going to fall back into sinful ways again. These are the ones who have gone to prison in more ways than one: spirit, soul and flesh. They were at one time on the dung pile of life.

3. The **IMPOSSIBLE ODDS ONES**: These are disciples who will face seemingly impossible odds that flesh and soul cannot overcome. Because Christ lives within their spirit the victories will be supernatural; God will bring them through every impossible situation.

I challenge you to be sold out to the Gospel and get out of the pew-warming, "member of the church" syndrome. Get actively involved in attacking the gates of hell. These gates cannot prevail against the good news sent from the throne room of God. We can reconcile all men to Jesus Christ if they are willing to receive him!

Are you willing to become a God-sent ambassador sharing grace and truth with the lost and hurting people of this world? The time is soon coming when the trumpet of God will sound and all mankind will have no more opportunity to accept or reject Jesus. **You and I are on a mission that is not impossible, for with God all things are possible through the blood of Jesus, His Son!**

EPILOGUE

A GOLD EL RENO STAR
by
Bruce Hunter

A day calmly draws to a close,
with sun waving fingers of beautiful trails.
Its golden shine warms the blue Okie sky
and leaves me abounding in colorful tales.
Memories serve well so I'm assured'ner again to be low'
cause God created and formed me, for this I'm ever to
know.
Oh yes, I sure miss family, friends, foe alike
for there's always a space...but never for spite.

One day I was a Star who was bold and so strong
but God's guidance and love I ran from so long.
Within was a craving for His world's carnal wealth
Satan saw, seized and led it with such devious stealth.
This bright, shiny star left its black, velvet sky
with much flash and bright streak it burned up with
anguished cry.

With anathema might police courts and tight chains
they did harness what pieces remained here to claim.
Into prison was sent, past all family and friends
cause this Star had outlived wild, crazy, new trends.
The night felt too dark, the days worse and drear
my hurt was so deep for approval was seared.
Yet within, I could sense my God drawing so near
His words from my childhood in silence could hear.

Purity or Prison

So, with purpose I determined to draw Him inside
For His words were so rich and flowed like strong tide.

A newness was wrought; peace, joy and Sonshine
as God spread His Son's fingers of love so divine.
This broken life, once racked with much pain from within
had life begin new with such rest from past sin.
Now Jesus Christ sheds words of joy in my life
Praise God, He came in to remove all the strife.
Committed to be God's harbinger of light to this world
with a message of hope through God's grace will unfurl.

God called me to preach when a lad on a beach
His Word filled with precepts and love I will teach.
Hallelujah, His Spirit quickens this fallen Star
to live holy and righteous in lands near and far.
Crossing lands and vast continents will travel and stand
to tell millions of Christ and His love; a Command.
There is coming a day when my family'll sure taste
for upon me God's hand is so mightily placed.
I, El Reno Star, who once left such scars
can now praise my God cause I'm called "His Gold Star."

◆

Undoubtedly, this book has placed each reader, you and me, into a greater focus of His light. You and I will never be the same. Over the years I have read many books, but there is one that has become dear to me. Oswald Chambers' daily devotional, _My Utmost for His Highest_ has become a favorite. As I end this book, may I share his words that have since become my daily desire.

Bruce Hunter

Since mine eyes have looked on Jesus
I've lost sight of all beside
So enchained my spirit's vision
Gazing on the crucified.

May God richly bless you as each day you contemplate
how your life may become the very pure vessel God
desires you to be. Truth will keep you pure and ultimately
prevent imprisonment within the spirit, soul and flesh.
You can remain pure and holy because the power of the
Holy Spirit is there to help you.

BRUCE HUNTER

Bruce was born and raised in South Africa. His parents were missionaries there for almost forty years. He is the father of three children; Chad, 24, a graduate of Wheaton College in Wheaton, Illinois, Shauna, 22, a senior at Southwest Missouri State University in Springfield, MO. and Trent, 19, a sophomore at Oral Roberts University in Tulsa, OK.

Bruce completed high school in Florida, South Africa. He was President (Head Boy), LEADER OF THE ROTC PROGRAM of his school and played rugby for many years with distinction on a national team. While he was studying at the university in South Africa he worked with a CPA firm as an auditor. In 1970 Bruce moved to the United States and by 1971 graduated from Evangel College, Springfield, MO. with a BA in Business Management and a minor in Economics.

Bruce entered business as a securities dealer, mortgage broker, insurance and financial consultant, franchising consultant and by 1987, became the president of a publicly traded company and owned prostate and impotency diagnostic medical clinics.

Bruce completed two Masters Degrees; Theology and Divinity and is now working on his dissertation for a doctorate in Theology.

Bruce is currently working on a sequel to this book planning for its release in May 1999. It will be titled, *THE HIDE AND SEEK OF SECRET HURTS.*

To order additional copies of *PURITY OR PRISON*, complete the information below.

Ship To: (please print)

Name_____

Address_____

City, State, Zip_____

Day Phone_____

_____copies of *Purity or Prison* @ $14.95 each $_____
      Postage and handling @ $2.50 per book $_____
      Total Amount enclosed $_____

Make checks payable to **Life In Christ Ministry** and mail to the address below.

Bruce Hunter is a prophetic teacher with a heart to stir people to righteousness. Bruce is currently pioneering a church in San Marcos, California. He travels and speaks at various seminars, conference, churches, schools, prisons, etc.

If you would like Bruce to book a speaking engagement, contact him through the following address:

L.I.C.M.
197 Woodland PKWY.
PMB 579
San Marcos, CA 92069

TEL: (760) 489-0790